What Your Colleagues Are Saying

"This is a bold book. . . . Its genius, and its unique contribution, is in bringing the balance and the centeredness to this new game in town—the Common Core, with so much potential to decenter us and upset our equilibrium."

—P. DAVID PEARSON
University of California Berkeley

"One would think that the first place to look when wanting information about the Common Core State Standards would be, well, the Common Core State Standards. The fact is, though, Doug Fisher and Nancy Frey are quickly becoming the go-to folks for information on teaching these standards. They've proven this again in *Rigorous Reading*. This is certainly a book to be added to your collection of books that attend to the demands of the CCSS."

—KYLENE BEERS, EdD

"With *Rigorous Reading,* Doug Fisher and Nancy Frey have provided literacy educators who are committed to successfully raising the bar with solutions that make sense. The book is masterfully developed with an extensive reach across many grade levels in terms of defining what it means to provide intentional instruction and teaching text complexity. The five access points are discussed pragmatically with evidence of a solid research base deftly woven throughout the book. This is the most practical book I have come across in terms of providing teachers with the knowledge base and assistance many are seeking to improve their instruction with regard to complex texts."

—STEVEN L. LAYNE, EdD
Professor of Literacy Education, Judson University
and Author of *Igniting a Passion for Reading*

"In *Rigorous Reading: 5 Access Points for Comprehending Complex Texts,* Fisher and Frey help teachers understand how to bring vigor to rigor. They teach us how to help students understand more from their complex texts—greater understanding that will help to bring life and energy to each student's reading. Rooted in solid research, this is book is a must-read for those grappling with how to translate the recommendations and mandates around text complexity from the Common Core into instructional practices."

—JENNIFER SERRAVALLO
Author of *Teaching Reading in Small Groups* and *Conferring with Readers*

"In a time when nearly every state has adopted the Common Core State Standards (CCSS), we need resources that show us how to support students in developing their full literacy potential. In this very practical and insightful book, Fisher and Frey examine how CCSS conceptions of text complexity are causing us to shift some of our ideas about reading instruction. *Rigorous Reading* is an important resource that will help teachers align reading instruction with the CCSS in powerful ways."

—LINDA B. GAMBRELL
Professor, Clemson University

RIGOROUS
READING

RIGOROUS READING

5 Access Points for Comprehending Complex Texts

NANCY FREY
DOUGLAS FISHER

FOREWORD BY P. DAVID PEARSON

CL CORWIN LITERACY

CORWIN
A SAGE Company

FOR INFORMATION:

Corwin

A SAGE Company

2455 Teller Road

Thousand Oaks, California 91320

(800) 233-9936

www.corwin.com

SAGE Publications Ltd.

1 Oliver's Yard

55 City Road

London EC1Y 1SP

United Kingdom

SAGE Publications India Pvt. Ltd.

B 1/I 1 Mohan Cooperative Industrial Area

Mathura Road, New Delhi 110 044

India

SAGE Publications Asia-Pacific Pte. Ltd.

3 Church Street

#10-04 Samsung Hub

Singapore 049483

Publisher: Lisa Luedeke

Development Editor: Julie Nemer

Editorial Assistant: Francesca Dutra Africano

Production Editor: Melanie Birdsall

Copy Editor: Matthew Sullivan

Typesetter: C&M Digitals (P) Ltd.

Proofreader: Caryne Brown

Indexer: Sheila Bodell

Cover Designer: Janet Kiesel

Graphic Designer: Gail Buschman

Copyright © 2013 by Corwin

Printed in the United States of America.

Library of Congress Cataloging-in-Publication Data

Frey, Nancy.

Rigorous reading: 5 access points for comprehending complex texts / Nancy Frey, Douglas Fisher.

pages cm

Includes bibliographical references and index.

ISBN 978-1-4522-6813-2 (pbk.)

1. Reading comprehension. I. Fisher, Douglas. II. Title.

LB1050.45.F74 2013

372.47—dc23   2013017528

This book is printed on acid-free paper.

16 17 18 10 9 8 7 6 5

Contents

CHAPTER 4. Access Point Three: Collaborative Conversations 73

CHAPTER 5. Access Point Four: An Independent Reading Staircase 97

CHAPTER 6. Access Point Five: Demonstrating Understanding and Assessing Performance 121

Visit the companion website at
www.corwin.com/rigorousreading
for access to the video clips,
Professional Learning Guide, and other resources.

■ ■ ■

Note From the Publisher: *The authors have provided video and web content throughout the book which is available to you through QR Codes. To read a QR Code, you must have a smartphone or tablet with a camera. We recommend that you download a QR Code reader app that is made specifically for your phone or tablet brand.*

QR Codes may provide access to videos and/or websites that are not maintained, sponsored, endorsed, or controlled by Corwin. Your use of these third-party websites will be subject to the terms and conditions posted on such websites. Corwin takes no responsibility and assumes no liability for your use of any third-party website. Corwin does not approve, sponsor, endorse, verify, or certify information available at any third-party video or website.

List of Videos

Access the following videos at **www.corwin.com/rigorousreading**.

Chapter 1

Video 1.1 Doug discusses text complexity.

Video 1.2 Nancy reviews a text for the factors of complexity.

Video 1.3 Doug discusses close reading.

Video 1.4 Teacher modeling comprehension strategies.

Video 1.5 Doug talks about the gradual release of responsibility.

Chapter 2

Video 2.1 A teacher models for her students.

Video 2.2 An elementary teacher models word solving.

Video 2.3 A high school teacher models word solving.

Video 2.4 A collection of purpose statements in elementary classrooms.

Video 2.5 A collection of purpose statements in secondary classrooms.

Video 2.6 Making sure students know the purpose.

Video 2.7 Complex texts and standards.

Chapter 3

Video 3.1 Close reading with sixth-grade English language learners.

Video 3.2 Students rereading and discussing a complex text in high school English.

Video 3.3 Close reading of historical information.

Video 3.4 Close reading and text-dependent questions in upper elementary school.

Video 3.5 Close reading in the primary grades.

Foreword

As I read *Rigorous Reading: 5 Access Points for Comprehending Complex Texts* by Nancy Frey and Doug Fisher, I kept searching for a metaphor or literary allusion to capture my stance toward this wonderful book. Several candidates came to mind . . .

▶ Forewarned Is Forearmed

This emphasizes the idea that Nancy and Doug are giving readers fair warning about what's coming up for teachers with the Common Core as the new sheriff in town.

▶ Knowledge Is Power

The connection here is the idea that Nancy and Doug operate from the principle that if teachers want to get ahead of the CCSS curve in curriculum, teaching, and assessment, then knowledge is the ultimate—indeed, the only—resource they can rely on. The more teachers know about comprehension and composition, the better equipped they—and hence their students—will be to handle the curves of the Common Core.

▶ Something Old, Something New, Something Borrowed, Something Blue

I landed on this traditional bridal apparel advice to emphasize the idea that in this book, as in all their books, Nancy and Doug (a) build on the past (the old) on their way to the future (the new), (b) incorporate elements of the work of others in their practices (something borrowed), and (c) make us aware of the dilemmas and constraints (the blue) that are always around to push back in the face of reform. But the blue piece seemed a little pessimistic for a Frey and Fisher book, for Nancy and Doug are nothing if they aren't optimistic about our collective and individual power as teachers to make a difference. Finally I settled on a variation of the apparel advice, one that is a little more upbeat:

▶ Something New, Something Old, Something Borrowed, Something Bold

This variation was a perfect fit. The new, the old, and the borrowed are surely there, but it's the bold that captures the essence of the book. This is a bold book, especially among the set of books offering advice about what to do in the wake of the Common Core. Many of us, myself included, are being circumspect about how enthusiastically we should accept new ideas like close reading, the staircase of text complexity, and productive failure. But Nancy and Doug have found a way to embrace these new ideas while maintaining their consistently strong commitment to meeting the individual needs of students and respecting the professional choices of teachers.

Something New

No question, it is their embrace of key elements of the Common Core implementation (close reading, upping the ante in text complexity, and productive failure) that is both *new* and *bold*. A whole chapter is devoted to how to do close reading well, including a lot of advice about crafting questions that require readers to "stay close to the text." I especially like the fact that they are clear about the idea that close reading does not equal literal, factual comprehension. They illustrate how to ask inferential, author's craft, comparative (across multiple texts), and critical reading questions that, along with literal, *all* require close reading of the text to generate a plausible answer. If teachers follow the advice here, they will end up with a balanced diet of text-based reading activities. Frey and Fisher rightfully point out that many of the abuses of the personal response probes that dominated the '80s and '90s resulted in interesting, engaging discussions in which the text was conscientiously avoided by everyone, including the teacher. This abuse, which I like to call wallowing at the trough of prior knowledge, deserves to be corrected to ensure the text plays a strong evidentiary role in all discussions, even those focused on interpretation and application. Frey and Fisher offer good advice about how to make this happen.

They also point out that a group of readers could traverse the text with many close readings. One might focus on a clear explication of the basic elements of a story or the key ideas in an explanatory text. A second might focus on author's craft, noting the various tools, like word choice or rhetorical frames (problem-solution or conflict-resolution), that authors use to shape the way readers understand text. The notion of second and third reads is a powerful tool for deepening and sharpening student understandings of text.

Something Old

In the process of focusing on the new world of the Common Core, Frey and Fisher do a great job of showing us how and why to deploy pedagogical tools that have become "old friends." Nowhere is this more evident that in the chapters on how to help students meet the challenge of reading of *even more* complex text than has been required of them in the past. Frey and Fisher show us how to use strategy instruction to equip students to manage the "clunks" of comprehension. They point out that much of the scaffolding that will allow students to meet complex texts where they are comes quite naturally from the collective expertise that is available when we all put our heads together in a collaborative reading activity. They further advise us that engaging kids in episodes of productive failure (e.g., trying to make sense out of really difficult texts) ought to happen in joint ventures rather than individual activities. The idea here is that when we "suffer through the experience together," we learn things from it, like that strategies can help us when the going gets tough, or that we can succeed in the face of imminent failure, that the resources of the group are greater than those available to any member of the group. They also find a place for routines of independent reading and individualized reading as key elements in supporting students on the staircase of text complexity, pointing out that ultimately students need to meet the text complexity challenge on their own.

Something Borrowed

Frey and Fisher books are good examples of intertextuality. They have a real knack for building on the theoretical perspectives and practical ideas that pervade the field and putting their own signature on them. That is part of what makes their texts so accessible to the rest of us. We encounter variations on themes that are at least partially familiar to us. But let me be clear: their work, their voice, is clearly Frey and Fisher's own unique contribution to the field; it's just that we can find many access points within that unique voice—professional pillows to land on if you will. It's a gift to be able to write like that. There are lots of examples of borrowed ideas in this book. To highlight a few—elements of different versions of guided and shared reading, emphasis on the importance of read-alouds (especially in doing close reading with younger and less independent readers), focusing on the purpose of the text (although they certainly bring a new twist to purpose setting), and a sensible and pared down approach to strategy instruction.

Something Bold

I already made the claim that much of what is new is also bold: their approach(es) to close reading and generating text-based questions, their suggestions for embracing a big increase in text complexity and productive failure, and their modifications of the role that we expect prior knowledge to play. But it is also bold of them to assert that there are roles for some variations of guided reading, personal response, and strategy instruction because we see so little talk about these practices in the implementation materials that have emerged in support of the Common Core.

▶ Something Balanced and Centered

One of the characteristics of the body of work that Frey and Fisher have brought to the field is that it is so centered in classrooms and schools (they write for teachers who work for kids and their families) and so balanced in terms of ALL of the goals of a truly comprehensive reading curriculum. This book is no exception to that characterization. It is both balanced and centered. Its genius and its unique contribution are in bringing the balance and the centeredness to this new game in town—the Common Core, with so much potential to decenter us and upset our equilibrium. Their advice will help us meet these new challenges while we maintain our balance, our center, and our commitment to the students and families who depend upon us to become ready for what life beyond school brings us, be it college, career, or just everyday life.

—*P. David Pearson*

Acknowledgments

We appreciate the National Association of Secondary School Principals (NASSP), and specifically Jan Umphrey (Editor of Principal Leadership), for the support of our work. We are pleased to be able to share some of the work we have done with NASSP with our readers here.

▶ Publisher's Acknowledgments

Corwin gratefully acknowledges the contributions of the following reviewers:

Sara K. Ahmed
The Bishop's School
La Jolla, CA

Maureen Connolly
The College of New Jersey
Ewing Township, NJ

Jennifer Serravallo
Teacher, Author, and Literacy Consultant
www.jenniferserravallo.com

Kym Sheehan
Literacy Consultant and Curriculum and Instruction Specialist
Port Charlotte, FL

Introduction: Your Access Point

Perhaps it was the title that caught your eye: *Rigorous Reading: 5 Access Points for Comprehending Complex Texts.* There are several phrases embedded in the title, any one of which could have resonated with you.

We chose *Rigorous Reading* because the language of the core standards has made it clear that our students are expected to engage regularly with complex texts. A first step toward doing so is in understanding exactly what makes a given text complex. Quantitative and qualitative measures of literary and informational texts are prompting our field to examine more closely the factors that contribute to text complexity. We stand on the shoulders of giants like William S. Gray, Jeanne Chall, Edward Fry, Elfrieda Hiebert, and so many others who have made it their lives' work to help us understand how a text works. In the past, we have been content to leave these determinations up to others. Now, we are ready to assume more responsibility for understanding what the numbers on the book cover mean. We are growing in our ability to perceive the nuances that make some texts more complex than others, especially in divining those qualities that only a knowledgeable human reader can perceive.

But knowing the breadth and depth of a text is not sufficient, and perhaps you picked up this book because the word *Comprehend* captured your attention. That's not surprising—did you know that reading comprehension studies are the oldest in the field of educational research? The earliest use of the term *comprehension* as it relates to reading was by J. Russell Webb in his *Normal Series of School Readers to Teach Correct Reading,* published in 1856. (By the way, the full title also promised to *Improve and Expand the Mind and Purify and Elevate the Character.*) Comprehension is fundamental in reading, and in this book. Without deep understanding, complex texts are inanimate objects. It is only in the reader's mind that a book comes to life. It is truly wondrous that the physical limitations of time and space vanish when a reader engages in silent dialogue with a writer. As teachers of reading, we want to share what Beatrix Potter imagined from her garden in the English countryside. As teachers of literacy in the disciplines, we want to make it possible for Aristotle's formal logic to come to life in the mind of a 21st century adolescent. Maybe J. Russell Webb was right after all.

Chances are good, though, that the phrase *Helping Students* was the clincher. The five access points we discuss in this book form its center. It would be woefully inadequate to simply fill a room with complex texts and believe that was enough. If it were, we could simply park our students for a decade or so in the great libraries in our schools and communities. But communing with Potter and Aristotle, not to mention Junot Diaz, Chinua Achebe, Basho, and Zu Chongzhi, is not possible without granting students access to these ideas. The five access points build a bridge between the reader and the text, and are accomplished through intentional instruction:

1. Establishing purpose for reading a complex text, and modeling how and expert reader (you) makes meaning
2. Providing scaffolded and close reading instruction to guide students through complex texts
3. Creating opportunities for collaborative conversations with peers to refine their understanding
4. Moving them forward through independent reading of increasingly complex texts
5. Using formative assessment opportunities so you and the reader know what is known, and what is not yet known

We wrote this book with access in mind, and our intention is to provide you with a road map for ensuring that all the students you work with, both now and in the future, can come to know what we collectively have known: The world of texts, whether print or digital, represents a history of our past and the promise of our future. Given that imperative, is there anything more important we can do than to open up access for children and adolescents? In a word—WELCOME.

Ramping Up for Complex Texts

1

Helping students read more and better has always been the goal of literacy educators. In our profession, we've tried all kinds of approaches to ensure that students can read and understand the wide range of texts they will be confronted with as they grow and develop. There have been times in our history when students were assigned to read hard texts independently. The thinking at the time was that exposure to great works alone would result in learned citizens. That didn't work because students found summaries that they could use to answer comprehension questions and write essays, although it certainly spawned a whole new publishing category: commercial study guides. Doug remembers being assigned to read *Antigone* and searching everywhere for CliffsNotes so that he could complete the required worksheets and write his essay in response to this prompt:

Identify the tragic hero of one of the plays. Analyze the scenes in which the character displays pride and identify the effects that this pride has on the character's life. How could his/her life have been different if he/she had behaved in a less prideful manner?

Just giving students complex text doesn't mean they will read and understand it.

Thankfully, the answers to this question were clearly articulated in the yellow- and black-striped book. It wasn't that Doug didn't want to read *Antigone*, but rather that although he was assigned to read it, he wasn't taught how to understand an ancient Greek play such that he could answer this prompt. Unfortunately, his teacher did not know that he hadn't read the play because he earned an A on the essay. Lesson learned: Just giving students complex text doesn't mean they will read and understand it.

At other times, we've scaffolded so much that we removed the need for students to read altogether. That didn't work because students were not applying what they had learned to new texts. Nancy remembers a teacher telling her class so much about each assigned chapter of *The Secret Garden* that Nancy didn't feel the need read the book at all, and spent her time reading Nancy Drew mysteries instead. She was able to complete all of the tasks (and please her teacher) because the teacher did the majority of the work. The fact that Nancy participated eagerly in classroom discussions wasn't an indication that she was a good reader but rather that she was a good listener. Her teacher's recounting of the previous night's chapter was sufficient for Nancy to engage in rich and collaborative discussions.

Neither of these approaches met the intended goal of getting students to read complex texts. Instead, they relied on either too little, or too much, teaching. To ensure that students actually do learn to read complex texts, teachers have to scaffold instruction and know when to transfer the cognitive and metacognitive responsibility to students. They need to rethink the texts they use, expanding the range to include more complex texts accompanied by scaffolds and support. And they need to carefully consider the intentional instruction students need to receive if they are going to apply what they have learned to the wide world of texts available to them.

In this chapter, we focus on two major concepts in literacy instruction: text complexity and close reading. Perhaps you work in a place where Common Core State Standards are the *lingua franca*; perhaps not. In either case, you are concerned with making it possible for students to read increasingly complex texts and to gain exposure to thoughtful reading instruction that provides access to these texts. Therefore, the first section will address text complexity and the impact of reading anchor standard 10. The second section will examine the call for students to read these texts closely, as described in reading anchor standard 1. These two standards are bookends for the remaining reading standards on our instructional bookshelf. The final portion of the chapter is an introduction to a gradual release of responsibility instructional framework that provides the access points students require to access complex texts.

▶ Reading Complex Texts: Anchor Standard 10

The Common Core State Standards for the English Language Arts have had a significant impact on the way educators are discussing reading instruction. This repositioning is having a ripple effect beyond the states currently committed to using these standards, as professional discourse is not contained by geographical boundaries. Nowhere is this more apparent than in the ongoing conversations about the use of complex texts. Anchor standard 10 is deceptively simple in theory: "Read and comprehend literary and informational texts independently and proficiently." It is proving to be much more complicated in practice (National Governors Association [NGA], 2010, p. 10). Expectations by grade level for this anchor standard can be found in Figure 1.1.

Let's parse out the anchor standard further to better understand its implications. *Read and comprehend* serves as a reminder that the ability to make meaning is the ultimate goal, and that carefully crafted instruction on decoding and comprehension strategies are fundamental. *Literary and informational texts* include a wide range of genres and text types, both digital and print. So far, so good—we can't imagine any literacy educator disagreeing with either of these parts of the goal.

It is the last phrase that has stirred debate—*independently and proficiently.* While everyone agrees that we shouldn't just hand students hard texts and

> *To ensure that students actually do learn to read complex texts, teachers have to scaffold instruction and know when to transfer the cognitive and metacognitive responsibility to students.*

Figure 1.1 Anchor Standard 10: Read and comprehend complex literary and informational texts independently and proficiently.

Grade	Expectations for Literature	Expectations for Informational Texts
12	By the end of grade 12, read and comprehend literature, including stories, dramas, and poems, at the high end of the grades 11–CCR text complexity band independently and proficiently.	By the end of grade 12, read and comprehend literary nonfiction at the high end of the grades 11–CCR text complexity band independently and proficiently.
11	By the end of grade 11, read and comprehend literature, including stories, dramas, and poems, in the grades 11–CCR text complexity band proficiently, with scaffolding as needed at the high end of the range.	By the end of grade 11, read and comprehend literary nonfiction in the grades 11–CCR text complexity band proficiently, with scaffolding as needed at the high end of the range.
10	By the end of grade 10, read and comprehend literature, including stories, dramas, and poems, at the high end of the grades 9–10 text complexity band independently and proficiently.	By the end of grade 10, read and comprehend literary nonfiction at the high end of the grades 9–10 text complexity band independently and proficiently.
9	By the end of grade 9, read and comprehend literature, including stories, dramas, and poems, in the grades 9–10 text complexity band proficiently, with scaffolding as needed at the high end of the range.	By the end of grade 9, read and comprehend literary nonfiction in the grades 9–10 text complexity band proficiently, with scaffolding as needed at the high end of the range.
8	By the end of the year, read and comprehend literature, including stories, dramas, and poems, at the high end of grades 6–8 text complexity band independently and proficiently.	By the end of the year, read and comprehend literary nonfiction at the high end of the grades 6–8 text complexity band independently and proficiently.
7	By the end of the year, read and comprehend literature, including stories, dramas, and poems, in the grades 6–8 text complexity band proficiently, with scaffolding as needed at the high end of the range.	By the end of the year, read and comprehend literary nonfiction in the grades 6–8 text complexity band proficiently, with scaffolding as needed at the high end of the range.
6	By the end of the year, read and comprehend literature, including stories, dramas, and poems, in the grades 6–8 text complexity band proficiently, with scaffolding as needed at the high end of the range.	By the end of the year, read and comprehend literary nonfiction in the grades 6–8 text complexity band proficiently, with scaffolding as needed at the high end of the range.

Grade	Expectations for Literature	Expectations for Informational Texts
5	By the end of the year, read and comprehend literature, including stories, dramas, and poetry, at the high end of the grades 4–5 text complexity band independently and proficiently.	By the end of the year, read and comprehend informational texts, including history/social studies, science, and technical texts, at the high end of the grades 4–5 text complexity band independently and proficiently.
4	By the end of the year, read and comprehend literature, including stories, dramas, and poetry, in the grades 4–5 text complexity band proficiently, with scaffolding as needed at the high end of the range.	By the end of year, read and comprehend informational texts, including history/social studies, science, and technical texts, in the grades 4–5 text complexity band proficiently, with scaffolding as needed at the high end of the range.
3	By the end of the year, read and comprehend literature, including stories, dramas, and poetry, at the high end of the grades 2–3 text complexity band independently and proficiently.	By the end of the year, read and comprehend informational texts, including history/social studies, science, and technical texts, at the high end of the grades 2–3 text complexity band independently and proficiently.
2	By the end of the year, read and comprehend literature, including stories and poetry, in the grades 2–3 text complexity band proficiently, with scaffolding as needed at the high end of the range.	By the end of year, read and comprehend informational texts, including history/social studies, science, and technical texts, in the grades 2–3 text complexity band proficiently, with scaffolding as needed at the high end of the range.
1	With prompting and support, read prose and poetry of appropriate complexity for grade 1.	With prompting and support, read informational texts appropriately complex for grade 1.
K	Actively engage in group reading activities with purpose and understanding.	Actively engage in group reading activities with purpose and understanding.

wish them well, the practice of scaffolded instruction is receiving renewed attention. How much is too much? When is it not enough? The Common Core State Standards for reading address this briefly with respect to the primary grades, noting that adult support and guidance are a part of the equation. But mention of this type of support disappears after grade 2. This may be due in part to the developers' position that the standards are not meant to dictate how students are taught—that they are, instead, intended to define the outcomes of the instruction.

The waters have been muddied a bit by the release of the publishers' criteria statements, first in 2011 and then again in 2012 with the revision that came out after portions of it were hotly challenged by a variety of professional groups. The revised statement takes into consideration the topic of scaffolding, noting "some students will need more scaffolding . . . Curriculum developers and teachers have the flexibility to build progressions of texts of increasing complexity within grade-level bands that overlap to a limited degree with earlier bands" (Coleman & Pimentel, 2012, p. 3). There is a deep body of research (e.g., Vygotsky, 1978; Wood, Bruner, & Ross, 1976; Wood & Wood, 1996) on the importance of scaffolding in instruction; we are pleased to see it more explicitly acknowledged in this statement.

While everyone agrees that we shouldn't just hand students hard texts and wish them well, the practice of scaffolded instruction is receiving renewed attention. How much is too much? When is it not enough?

Scaffolded instruction is vital in reading instruction, and its practice is universal. Scaffolding in reading instruction occurs through the use of texts (Fountas & Pinnell, 2012), strategically deployed questions, prompts and cues (Frey & Fisher, 2010), and a gradient of instructional arrangements (Fisher & Frey, 2008; Pearson & Gallagher, 1983). Each of these dimensions of curriculum and instruction is essential for teaching students how to read, and for building their capacity to read for meaning. For students to access complex text, their reading experiences must include a thoughtful progression of texts, scaffolds, and instructional arrangements.

A second dimension of the phrase *independently and proficiently* concerns exactly what students should be reading. The easy response is "grade-level texts, of course," but what exactly constitutes "grade level"? Teachers have operated under tacit agreements about grade level, often relying on local context and traditions. Haven't we all worked in schools where a particular title was considered the province of a specific grade level? For example, where we live, *Charlotte's Web* is third grade, and *Romeo and Juliet* is ninth grade. However, in many cases, these traditions seemed to be justified primarily because units and materials had already been developed and shifting the book to another grade was too much trouble. The game-changing nature of the documentation that accompanies this anchor standard is that for the first time, "grade level" is being defined quite clearly. Citing research on the gap between graduating seniors' reading levels and those expected for college freshmen, the developers wrote the standards specifically to close this gap. To do so, they have called for the use of complex texts that continually stretch students' capacity to read and comprehend literary and informational texts. In other words, the expectation is that students will read and understand more complex texts than they have been expected to in the past. But to what end—and how do we know what makes a text complex?

▶ A New Definition of Text Complexity

In the past, text complexity and readability were viewed interchangeably by many practitioners, even as researchers cautioned otherwise (Hiebert, 2009). Readability has been estimated based on the average length of sentences, the number of syllables in sentences, and—in some cases—occurrences of rare words. These measures provided teachers with general information about readability and were used to gauge appropriate materials for students. But many have voiced concern that these measures missed the nuances present in many texts, often reporting readings as being easier than they really were. Works by Ernest Hemingway, for example, have been assigned a difficulty level ranging from grades 4 to 8, yet any teacher who has used his works of literature knows that the concepts, dialogue, and background knowledge needed by the reader make these texts far more complex than can be measured by a readability formula alone.

Drawing on the extensive research on the measurement and characteristics of text, the developers of the Common Core State Standards (NGA, 2010) identified three inter-related aspects of determining text complexity: quantitative evaluation, qualitative evaluation, and consideration of the reader and tasks. The authors define each of these as follows:

- **Quantitative evaluation:** readability measures and other scores of text complexity
- **Qualitative evaluation:** levels of meaning, structure, language conventionality and clarity, and knowledge demands
- **Matching readers with texts and tasks:** reader variables (such as motivation, knowledge, and experiences) and task variables (such as purpose and the complexity generated by the task assigned and the questions posed) (p. 57)

Text analysis must always keep all three elements in mind.

Quantitative Evaluation

The temptation is to rely on the quantitative measures alone, which are derived from algorithms that yield numerical data; these measures can be

Video 1.1

Doug discusses text complexity. *www.corwin.com/ rigorousreading*

calculated by a computer and do an adequate job of tentatively placing a text within a grade band. But these measures alone are inadequate for understanding why one piece of text is qualitatively more difficult than another with the same quantitative score. It is simply insufficient to use readability data (sentence length, use of rare words, and such) and assume that this is the only information needed for gauging text complexity. Furthermore, you can't derive much guidance in terms of your teaching points from quantitative analysis alone. The art of making meaningful qualitative evaluations is best left to the judgment of a knowledgeable educator who is deeply familiar with the texts in question.

For students to access complex text, their reading experiences must include a thoughtful progression of texts, scaffolds, and instructional arrangements.

Qualitative Evaluation

Qualitative evaluation requires considering a text across four dimensions: levels of meaning and purpose, structure, language convention and clarity, and knowledge demands (see Figure 1.2). Note that these descriptors mirror the teaching points we rely on during instruction. A given text is going to be variously more or less difficult within each of these areas, and it is unlikely that any text would be uniformly difficult across all four. Structure refers to the genre of the text, its organization and narration, the number of text features, and its use of graphics (if applicable). The *Magic School Bus* series of science stories, for instance, is made more accessible because it uses a narrative structure of a group of children and their teacher on field trips to explain complex topics. On the other hand, *Night* (Wiesel, 1982) uses a difficult structure—flashback—that can confuse readers.

A second dimension of qualitative measures of text complexity concerns levels of meaning. Some texts are straightforward in their presentation of information, while others use figurative language, or present dense and complex ideas. For example, the informational picture book *How Artists See Families* (Carroll, 1997) is less complex in terms of levels of meaning, as it explains each image in concrete and observable terms. While quantitatively easier, the picture book *Frida* (Winter, 2002), with its ambiguous and unexplained images reminiscent of Frida Kahlo's work, requires readers to understand the story on two levels.

The degree to which the language conventions are similar to or different from those commonly understood can also affect complexity. Hesse's use of font size and sentence grammar variants to represent her protagonist's cognitive processes in *Music of the Dolphins* (1996) conveys the story's message

Video 1.2

Nancy reviews a text for the factors of complexity.
www.corwin.com/ rigorousreading

Figure 1.2 Qualitative Factors of Text Complexity

Component	Aspects	When a text is complex . . .
Levels of Meaning and Purpose	• Density and complexity	Many ideas come at the reader, or there are multiple levels of meaning, some of which are not clearly stated.
	• Figurative language	There are many literary devices (e.g., metaphors, personification) or devices that the reader is not familiar with (e.g., symbolism, irony) as well as idioms or clichés.
	• Purpose	Either the purpose is not stated or is purposefully withheld. The reader has to determine the theme or message.
Structure	• Genre	The genre is unfamiliar or the author bends the rules of the genre.
	• Organization	It does not follow traditional structures such as problem/solution, cause/effect, compare/contrast, sequence or chronology, and rich descriptions.
	• Narration	The narrator is unreliable, changes during the course of the text, or has a limited perspective for the reader.
	• Text features	Fewer signposts such as headings, bold words, margin notes, font changes, or footnotes are used.
	• Graphics	Visual information is not repeated in the text itself but the graphics or illustrations are essential to understanding the main ideas.
Language Conventionality and Clarity	• Standard English and variations	Variations of standard English, such as regional dialects or vernaculars that the reader is not familiar with, are included.
	• Register	It is archaic, formal, scholarly, or fixed in time.
Knowledge Demands	• Background knowledge	The demands on the reader extend well beyond his or her personal life experience.
	• Prior knowledge	The demands on the reader extend well beyond what he or she has been formally taught in school.
	• Cultural knowledge	The demands on the reader extend well beyond his or her cultural experiences and may include references to archaic or historical cultures.
	• Vocabulary	The words used are representations of complex ideas that are unfamiliar to the reader or they are domain specific and not easily understood using context clues or morphological knowledge.

of a growing awareness and then rejection of human ways by a girl raised by dolphins. By comparison, *The Grouchy Ladybug* (Carle, 1996) carries the same quantitative measure (a Lexile score of 560) but tells a far simpler story using familiar language conventions.

Finally, the relative knowledge demanded of the reader plays into the level of complexity of a given text. Doug's difficulty with *Antigone* stemmed from the fact that it requires the reader to have a vast amount of cultural knowledge, in this case of ancient Greek mythology, to make sense of the text. By comparison, *Dateline: Troy* (Fleischman, 2006) recounts portions of the *Iliad* by comparing it to modern news and gossip stories. In this way, elements of the Trojan War are made familiar by comparing them to 20th century wars. Both texts feature major archetypes in literature, but whereas the first requires the reader to recognize them, the second assumes that the reader doesn't already know them and instead draws attention to them more overtly.

Matching Readers With Texts and Tasks

Quantitative and qualitative dimensions are solely about the characteristics of the book itself. The third facet in determining text complexity, however, is about the match between reader, text, and task. This last facet is

where teaching lies, and in fact is the central theme of this book. We will return to this throughout these chapters, but for now, we want to consider the interaction between the reader and the text. There are myriad books to select from (over 328,000 new titles published in the U.S. in 2010), but only a few will make their way to your classroom or school. Some have worried that the core standards represent a retreat to a rigid approach of text explication and objective analysis that marked secondary English instruction in the mid-20th century. But the more progressive notion of including the reader when determining text complexity offers a counterpoint to that concern. This idea is drawn from Louise Rosenblatt's (2003) research on reader response theory. Her groundbreaking work has informed many other perspectives, including critical literacy (McLaughlin, & DeVoogd, 2004) and multicultural education (Banks & Banks, 2012). In addition to meeting the criteria of complexity, proponents of reader response theory argue that the texts you select should

In the past, text complexity and readability were viewed interchangeably by many practitioners, even as researchers cautioned otherwise.

- provide students with examples of quality writing that mentor them as writers themselves;
- grant students access to excellent illustrations;
- allow students to see themselves–their religion, ethnicity, language, and culture—in the selected texts;
- permit students to interact—through the act of reading—with people who have different experiences and beliefs;
- depict a variety of family structures;
- offer a balanced portrayal of gender identities and roles in terms of the depiction of the characters and what the characters do; and
- interrupt gender, racial, or ability stereotypes.

Another way to find quality books is to review titles that have received national and international recognition. For example, the American Library Association awards the Newbery (for writing) and the Caldecott (for illustration) each year for the best children's books. The same organization presents the Coretta Scott King award to outstanding African-American authors and illustrators of books for children and young adults. The University of Texas offers the Tomás Rivera award to for children's books that depict the Mexican-American experience. The Orbus Pictus award is given by the National Council of Teachers of English for outstanding nonfiction written for children. The Hans Christian Andersen medal is presented biennially by the International Board of Books for Young People in recognition of the body of work of an author and of an illustrator. Each state awards a series of young reader medals for books that are particularly popular with students in the state. The state reading association or library association will have a list of these awards by year. In addition, the International Reading Association created the Children's Choice, Teen Choice, and Teachers' Choices awards.

Understanding the quantitative and qualitative properties of texts is essential, as are the considerations regarding the interaction between the reader and the text. While these are helpful categories, they do not provide instructional guidance for teachers hoping to build their students' comprehension of the texts. What do we do with complex texts once we have them? It's important to remember that there is no evidence that students can learn from books they can't read (Allington, 2002). When it comes to reading challenging texts, students must be adequately supported to unlock the meanings hidden within.

▶ Reading Closely: Anchor Standard 1

An examination of reading anchor standard 1 further illuminates this question. It requires students to "[r]ead closely to determine what the text says explicitly and to make logical inferences from it; cite specific textual evidence when writing or speaking to support conclusions drawn from the text" (NGA, 2010, p. 10). This requires students to stay close to the text to build a solid foundation of textual knowledge. Grade-level expectations for this standard can be found in Figure 1.3. Note that the expectations for narrative and informational texts are the same for this standard, but that they differed for anchor standard 10. Anchor standards 2–9 provide teachers with information about what elements students should be able to leverage when analyzing complex texts:

Quantitative measures alone are inadequate for understanding why one piece of text is qualitatively more difficult than another.

- Themes and central ideas (standard 2)
- Characters and individuals (standard 3)
- Vocabulary (standard 4)
- Text structure (standard 5)
- Point of view (standard 6)
- Integration of content within and across text formats (standard 7)
- Arguments and reasoning (standard 8)
- Intertextual connections (standard 9)

In other words, anchor standard 10 encourages educators to examine the types of texts used, whereas standard 1 reminds us to fully mine the text for all it has to offer. These serve as bookends for the remaining reading standards, which describe the facets of reading comprehension that are essential for higher-order thinking and critical analysis. The intention is

Figure 1.3 Anchor Standard 1: Read closely to determine what the text says explicitly and to make logical inferences from it; cite specific textual evidence when writing or speaking to support conclusions drawn from the text.

Grade	Expectations for Literature and Informational Texts
11–12	Cite strong and thorough textual evidence to support analysis of what the text says explicitly as well as inferences drawn from the text, including determining where the text leaves matters uncertain.
9–10	Cite strong and thorough textual evidence to support analysis of what the text says explicitly as well as inferences drawn from the text.
8	Cite the textual evidence that most strongly supports an analysis of what the text says explicitly as well as inferences drawn from the text.
7	Cite several pieces of textual evidence to support analysis of what the text says explicitly as well as inferences drawn from the text.
6	Cite textual evidence to support analysis of what the text says explicitly as well as inferences drawn from the text.
5	Quote accurately from a text when explaining what the text says explicitly and when drawing inferences from the text.
4	Refer to details and examples in a text when explaining what the text says explicitly and when drawing inferences from the text.
3	Ask and answer questions to demonstrate understanding of a text, referring explicitly to the text as the basis for the answers.
2	Ask and answer such questions as who, what, where, when, why, and how to demonstrate understanding of key details in a text.
1	Ask and answer questions about key details in a text.
K	With prompting and support, ask and answer questions about key details in a text.

to drive students deeper into the text, and not simply draw on the surface comprehension many have grown accustomed to in classrooms.

Much attention has been given to the process of close reading, which relies on repeated readings of short passages of complex texts. A key purpose of close reading is to encourage students to examine in detail what the text has to say. The first assumption behind the practice of close reading is that the text is worthy; not everything we read requires this kind of inspection. However, understanding the text itself is necessary for comprehension and is key to making the kind of analytic and evaluative judgments that mark a competent reader. One question we often hear is in regard to the use of close reading practices with students who are not yet fully independent readers. It is helpful to keep in mind that the intent of close reading is to foster critical thinking skills to deepen comprehension. Therefore, the thinking skills needed for close reading should begin in kindergarten. Although the delivery of the lesson is somewhat different when working with emergent readers, the intention is the same. The use of close reading in primary grades will be discussed in greater detail in Chapter 3.

We apply the same reasoning when working with students with disabilities. It is essential that they receive access to general curriculum, as stated in both federal law and widely accepted best practices. Our experiences have shown us that close reading is especially useful for these and other students for whom a "one and done" reading of a text is not sufficient. Close reading affords students with the gift of time to linger with a piece of text. While we have known for decades that multiple readings are essential for deep understanding, in practice, we have rarely afforded students with the time to do so. Some of the greatest gains we have witnessed in our own classrooms have been with students who have otherwise struggled as readers.

The art of making meaningful qualitative evaluations is best left to the judgment of a knowledgeable educator who is deeply familiar with the texts in question.

There has been debate about the role of activating prior knowledge in a close reading. Reading comprehension is not a skill that exists in a vacuum between the reader and the text immediately in front of her; it also hinges on the accumulation of the many texts and experiences that she has been exposed to throughout her lifetime (e.g., Rosenblatt, 2003). Therefore, a competent reader links her prior knowledge to the new information she is experiencing. We believe that thoughtful reading teachers must encourage students to analyze, make judgments, synthesize across multiple sources of information, formulate opinions, and create new products. To do this, they should be integrating what they have learned from the text with their prior knowledge and experiences. But we share the concern that, in too many cases, the rush to engage students in these critical thinking skills has meant that relatively little time is allocated for eyes on the text. Instead, after extensive pre-teaching of the content of the text by the teacher, the text is all too often given a quick once over. In these cases, true integration doesn't take place; instead, students are mostly drawing on what they already know. It's hard to make forward progress when you're mostly just treading water.

If students are going to access complex texts, they must been given the time to read and reread, to respond to questions that encourage them to return to the text, and to discuss their ideas in the company of others. A strong textual foundation also makes it possible for them to engage in critical thinking skills. It's analogous to a ladder: It doesn't matter how tall the ladder is if the lower rungs are not solid. In our own classrooms, we are witnessing what is happening with our students who struggle to read. We are finding that spending more time on the textual foundations—the lower rungs of the ladder—is making it possible for them to analyze, evaluate, and create.

Anchor standard 10 calls for regular exposure to complex texts, and anchor standard 1 reminds us that students need to read these texts closely to interpret them. Standards 2–9 are the ways we think about and understand the text we're reading and discussing. But developing readers are apprentices to the kinds of problem-solving strategies that expert readers use when their comprehension breaks down. When it comes to using complex text, expect comprehension to break down regularly, and seize the opportunities these breakdowns present. These are ideal for showing students how these problem-solving comprehension strategies are summoned so that, over time, they become a part of their repertoire as skilled readers (Afflerbach, Pearson, & Paris, 2008).

▶ The Importance of Comprehension Strategies Instruction for Accessing Complex Texts

The lights are out in Ms. Butler's fourth-grade classroom. Every eye is glued to the screen on which she has projected a website explaining the history of chocolate. She knows that the text is complex, as she had analyzed it earlier using the qualitative rubric at the end of this chapter. She identified that the prior knowledge needed, as well as the extensive use of metaphors (a function of figurative language) were especially challenging. She paired this information about the qualitative elements of the text with her knowledge of her students as readers. She had previously noticed that her students were not creating mental images as they read, which compromised their understanding of the texts they were reading. She decided to model this cognitive strategy for her students using a think-aloud and then asking them to apply their learning in small groups.

Ms. Butler reads the informational text aloud, pausing periodically to share her thinking about the text. At one point, she pauses and says,

> I see huge vats of chocolate melting and some guy standing there stirring the chocolate. I can just smell the sweetness of the chocolate as it melts. I'm picturing this in my mind so that I can create an image that will help me connect the information that the author wants me to remember.

These words are not in the text. Ms. Butler is describing her own mental visualizations so that her students will begin to do so on their own.

As she finishes the shared reading, having focused on the role chocolate has played in civilization and on visualization as a comprehension strategy, one group of students joins her for scaffolded reading instruction. All of the other students are engaged in collaborative conversations and peer learning activities. Ms. Butler knows that the students in this first group have difficulty with visualizing the text. She has selected an excerpt of *Charlie and the Chocolate Factory* by Roald Dahl (1964) to read with them. She knows that many of the students in this group have either read this book or will read this book after this lesson. However, that isn't her focus with them. The part of the book she has selected finds the group inside the chocolate factory looking at the chocolate river. She shares the passage with the group and asks each student to visualize as she reads. When she has finished, she asks for students to volunteer to share "the pictures in your minds."

Arturo volunteers to speak first and says, "I was looking down into the river, but I couldn't see anything because the chocolate was too thick." Sarah says, "The smell, ohh, that smell. I just can't stand it! It's too sweet. Who could eat that much chocolate?" Bryan adds, "I can feel it between my toes. It's almost like mud, but thicker. I try to splash the river with my feet, but the chocolate is so thick that it just moves around."

Some have worried that the core standards represent a retreat to a rigid approach of text explication and objective analysis that marked secondary English instruction in the mid-20th century.

Ms. Butler reads other passages about chocolate that she has identified from the book. Again, students share their visualizations. After about 20 minutes, she is satisfied with their progress and excuses the members of this group to the collaborative learning activities and invites another group of students to the table.

The Common Core State Standards do not explicitly call for comprehension strategy instruction. That does not mean that this type of instruction should be discontinued. The standards represent the desired outcomes against which progress can be measured at the end of the year to determine if students can read and understand complex texts. As such, they are not concerned with the approaches teachers use to prepare students. Of course teachers should model and guide students such that they develop a habit of automatically using these cognitive strategies. The problem in the past has been that the development of comprehension strategies has been seen as an outcome in and of itself. With the adoption of the Common Core State Standards, comprehension strategies are viewed as a path toward understanding and accessing complex texts.

What do we do with complex texts once we have them? When it comes to reading challenging texts, students must be adequately supported to unlock the meanings hidden within.

Comprehension strategies are taught to students of all developmental levels so that they may use them as tools to support their own understanding of a given text (e.g., Fisher, Lapp, & Frey, 2011). As with tools in a toolbox, the key to the usefulness of these strategies lies in how thoughtfully they are applied to suit a particular purpose. These strategies include the following:

- **Questioning strategies** to predict and anticipate what might occur next in the text, to solve problems, and to clarify textual understanding
- **Summarizing strategies** to identify important information and accurately recount a text
- **Inferencing strategies** to "read between the lines" to identify clues in the text
- **Self-monitoring strategies** to determine when readers understand what they have read and notice when they have not
- **Connection strategies** to integrate what a reader has experienced and has learned with the information being read

Video 1.4

Teacher modeling comprehension strategies.
www.corwin.com/ rigorousreading

- **Analysis strategies** to identify literary devices, determine the author's purpose, and evaluate texts

We believe there is a danger in teaching comprehension strategies in isolation of one another, which was a mistake commonly made in the past. Pinnell and Fountas (2003) remind us that

> [t]hese strategies are not linear in that first you engage one then another. In fact, reducing complex systems to a list . . . probably oversimplifies reading. *Teaching* strategies one at a time and telling students to consciously employ them, *one at a time,* may actually interfere with deep comprehension and make reading a meaningless exercise. (pp. 7–8)

Complex text instruction is an ideal opportunity to consolidate the many skills and strategies students are learning throughout their reading day. They locate information in the text, integrate it with their prior knowledge, and get to use comprehension strategies in real time to get themselves unstuck when understanding breaks down. The ability to coordinate all of these cognitive and metacognitive processes is not easy and requires a framework for instruction that doesn't leave students floundering alone.

▶ Accessing Complex Texts Through a Gradual Release of Responsibility

Video 1.5

Doug talks about the gradual release of responsibility. *www.corwin.com/ rigorousreading*

For students to access complex texts, they need intentional instruction that provides them with *access* to deep comprehension. In this book, we've identified five "access points," that is, five ways to intentionally guide students' comprehension of complex text. The framework that allows for the implementation of this type of intentional instruction is known as *gradual release of responsibility* (e.g., Fisher & Frey, 2008; Pearson & Fielding, 1991). In the remainder of this book, we describe in detail each access point, always through the lens of complex texts. The chapters are as follows:

- Chapter 2, "Access Point One: Purpose and Modeling," describes the first access point—establishing the purpose of the lesson, or the learning target—and explains the ways that teachers can model their critical thinking for students as they read. In this chapter, we discuss the use of think-alouds and interactive shared readings, with special attention on the modeling of annotation skills.

- Chapter 3, "Access Point Two: Close and Scaffolded Reading Instruction," describes the second access point: close reading and scaffolded reading instruction. The practice of close reading, which emphasizes repeated readings, discussion, and critical thinking, requires scaffolded instruction. Text-dependent questions, prompts, and cues form the basis of these scaffolds and provide students with the teacher-supported experiences they need to read increasingly complex texts.

- Chapter 4, "Access Point Three: Collaborative Conversations," describes the third access point: collaborative conversations. These peer-led learning experiences require tasks that encourage students to interact and to apply what they have learned through close reading to develop deeper understandings of complex texts. In this chapter, we discuss a number of ways that teachers can facilitate student-to-student collaboration, including literature circles, discussion roundtables, reciprocal teaching, and collaborative strategic reading.

- Chapter 5, "Access Point Four: An Independent Reading Staircase," focuses on students' ability to access a figurative reading staircase as they apply what they have learned and read increasingly complex texts independently. While they may be reading individually, they are not reading alone, and well-designed instruction is essential in this phase. This chapter explains how to craft this instruction through the use of texts that build background knowledge and through peer-conferencing strategies that foster metacognitive awareness.

- Chapter 6, "Access Point Five: Demonstrating Understanding and Assessing Performance," concerns itself with demonstrating understanding

It is helpful to keep in mind that the intent of close reading is to foster critical thinking skills to deepen comprehension.

and assessing performance. These practices are not only for the teacher to use when measuring mastery but also for students to use to propel future learning. This chapter focuses on what occurs after reading, including feedback and assessment.

Doug's and Nancy's teachers, however well meaning, didn't know how to use these access points. Doug's teacher released cognitive responsibility much too suddenly, and he was left to try to find an outside source of information because he didn't know how to locate it within the text. Nancy's teacher never released any of the responsibility and did too much of the cognitive heavy lifting for her students. The teacher's assessments focused on the wrong measures, and she never did figure out that Nancy hadn't read the book. In using a range of access points, teachers can avoid these all-too-common pitfalls and balance support with challenge.

Students should be integrating what they have learned from the text with their prior knowledge and experiences. But we share the concern that, in too many cases, the rush to engage students in these critical thinking skills has meant that relatively little time is allocated for eyes on the text.

▶ Summary

The Common Core State Standards spotlight complex texts as a chief means for elevating student learning. One method for measuring text complexity is quantitative and relies on the number and types of words in the text; this measure is useful for situating a text within a grade band. However, this method of measurement does not uncover the qualitative values that render a text more or less complex. These include levels of meaning and purpose, structure, language conventions and clarity, and knowledge demands. These values give us insight into *what* to teach. The third facet of complexity concerns the reader characteristics and task demands, which inform *how* we teach complex texts. As students read these texts closely, they need support and instruction on how to identify textual elements and mine texts for understanding, as well as on how to use comprehension strategies to repair meaning when it becomes muddled. The intention behind effective instruction is for students to expand their capacity to deeply understand these kinds of complex texts outside the company of their teachers. It is this understanding that lies at the heart of college and career readiness. By equipping students to take on an ever-widening range of texts, we afford them their independence and extend their understanding of and influence on the biological, social, and physical world around them.

Access Point One

Purpose and Modeling

M s. Carver asks her students to get out their copies of *Number the Stars* (Lowry, 1989) while she places her copy of the book on the document camera. "Boys and girls," she begins,

> Today we're going to think about the specific words that
> the author has chosen and practice asking questions while
> we read. I'm going to share some of my thinking with
> you, especially about the author's words and the questions
> I have when I am reading. I'll give you a chance to try it
> with your reading partner.

After leading a discussion of the plot thus far, she begins to read while students follow silently in their books (her thinking aloud is italicized).

> "Your names?" the officer barked.

"Annemarie Johansen. And this is my sister—"

"Quiet! Let her speak for herself. Your name?" He was glaring at Ellen. *"Barked" and "glaring" are words the author is using to help me imagine this Nazi officer's anger. The author's word choice is important and in this case helps me think about the seriousness of the situation.*

Ellen swallowed. "Lise," she said, and cleared her throat. "Lise Johansen." *I know why she's lying. She doesn't want them to know she's Jewish so she pretends to be a member of the family. I'll bet the Johansens will also lie for Ellen.*

The officer stared at them grimly. "Now," Mama said in a strong voice, "you have seen that we are not hiding anything. May my children go back to bed?" *I was right. That's just what Mrs. Johansen did.*

The officer ignored her. Suddenly he grabbed a handful of Ellen's hair. Ellen winced. *Why would he pull Ellen's hair?*

He laughed scornfully. "You have a blond child sleeping in the other room. And you have this blond daughter—" he gestured toward Annemarie with his head. "Where did you get the dark-haired one?" *Oh, no! What will the Johansens say? Now I understand why the title of this chapter is "Who Is the Dark-Haired One?"* (Lowry, 1989, pp. 46–47).

After discussing the content of the passage, she leads a discussion about the think-aloud. "What are the ways I helped myself to understand what was happening in the text?" she asks. Jerome offers, "You made predictions about what would happen next." Delia adds, "You asked questions, like when the Nazi pulled Ellen's hair." While students respond, Ms. Carver records their ideas on chart paper. When finished, the list reads,

- Analyze word choices
- Make predictions and confirmations
- Ask questions
- Make connections to the title
- Visualize
- Think about what we already know about a character

Accessing complex texts requires structured time for students to work through new strategies and practice skills.

She asks students to listen to the next portion of the text and make suggestions about predictive statements and questions. She pauses after every few sentences to prompt suggestions and writes their ideas on a second piece of chart paper. They continue to practice as a class using the next few pages of text. After several cycles of modeling and scaffolding, she asks students to work in pairs; each student will read a page from the book to the other while using think-aloud statements to support their comprehension.

Accessing complex texts requires structured time for students to work through new strategies and practice skills. Of course, students should know what they are expected to learn. A number of studies have found that when the teacher states objectives and provides feedback, student learning increases (Dean, Stone, Hubbell, & Pitler, 2012). However, while establishing purpose primes learning, it does not ensure that it will occur; priming is insufficient without further instruction. Simply telling students what they are to learn doesn't guarantee they will learn it. A second technique for helping students learn new concepts and skills includes modeling through demonstration, that is, stopping to emphasize the parts of a text that offer examples of the stated purpose. A planning template for purpose and modeling appears in Figure 2.1.

A number of studies have found that when the teacher states objectives and provides feedback, student learning increases.

There are a wide range of topics for which teachers can provide models. This book centers on the topic of complex texts. It is important to note that Ms. Carver did not select a text that her students could read independently or even one that they could read with a little assistance. She selected a complex text that required intentional instruction. As noted in the discussion about the lesson, there are places in a given complex text that require teacher modeling or thinking aloud. Other parts of the text might be approrpriate for close readings, collaborative conversations, partner reading, or independent reading. In the language of the Common Core State Standards, this is the third contributing element to text complexity—identifying the appropriate task for the text. To ensure that students can access complex texts, their teachers must first select complex texts and then model their thinking about the text. This type of teaching requires active involvement and shared responsibility between teachers and their students.

▶ Accessing Complex Text Requires Modeling

As Wilhelm (2001) notes, "[T]eachers model their thinking by voicing all the things they are noticing, doing, seeing, feeling, and asking as they

Figure 2.1   Planning for Purpose and Modeling
Assessed Need: I have noticed that the students in my classroom need to work on:
Standards:
Text I will use:
Materials needed for this lesson are:
Purpose of the lesson is:
Model • Parts to emphasize

Figure 2.1 (Continued)

Scaffold

- Questions to ask

Assess

- These are the students who need extra support

Practice

- Students will practice using the strategy or skill during

Reflection

- What did I notice about what my students understood?

- What did I notice about my students' misunderstandings?

process the text" (p. 26). In other words, the idea is that the teacher explicitly or intentionally models the strategies that readers can use as they read. It would be a mistake to rely solely on the language of the core standards for guidance in what should be modeled, as these are outcome statements and not descriptions of the more fine-grained progression of comprehension strategies we use in our teaching. All readers regularly fall back on strategies for resolving confusions when meaning breaks down. Once comprehension is regained, the reader continues. An important aspect of reading instruction is that we show students how and when to use these strategies when they get stuck. That's precisely why we don't want to excuse students who struggle to read from this kind of instruction. Arguably, they are the ones who can benefit the most from it. Because it is the teacher who is assuming most of the cognitive load during modeling, all students can access the text. To distance struggling students from this instruction is to magnify the difficulties they already possess. In other words, how would you learn to repair something if you were systematically excused every time someone began using a tool?

Teachers can model any number of things that they want their students to learn, from how to interact with peers to how to compose an essay. In this book, we're addressing the topic of accessing complex text, so we will focus our discussion of modeling around the factors that contribute to text complexity. At the beginning of this chapter, Ms. Carver focused on knowledge demands (specifically vocabulary) and levels of meaning (specifically, density and complexity) as she modeled from *Number the Stars*. She knew these elements would factor into her students' comprehension of the text, and she used a think-aloud process to give voice to the ways she maintained her understanding of the passage.

We want students to recognize that complex texts require more from us as readers than those readings that are a more comfortable fit. Novice readers make the mistake of approaching all texts as equivalent, when they are not. In too many cases, when the text is challenging, they turn away and give up. As an expert reader, you activate different processes depending on the level of complexity you encounter. You know that you'll need to make notes for yourself when you're reading a James Joyce novel with your book club. You know how to look up an unfamiliar tax code in the manual that accompanied your annual tax return

Video 2.1

A teacher models for her students.
www.corwin.com/ rigorousreading

forms. When you encounter an unknown term while reading about the side effects listed in your prescription medicine insert, you consult several trusted resources. Novice readers don't automatically do these things.

Modeling is a time when you highlight the areas that you predict will be difficult for students, and you show them how you resolve comprehension problems. In addition, it is an important opportunity to show them how you interact with complex text.

There are places in a given complex text that require teacher modeling or thinking aloud.

Below, we will further discuss five reasons for modeling and the methods for doing so:

- Model that which is difficult for students
- Model ways to resolve problems
- Model how you interact with text
- Model through think-alouds
- Model through interactive shared readings

Taken together, what you are really modeling are the habits of active readers when confronted with challenging text. You are modeling persistence and a willingness to stick with something more difficult because it's worth it.

Model That Which Is Difficult for Students

The first principle of modeling is that you are selective in what you model. There's not much point in modeling what students already know how to do, and in any case, it is not going to provide them with access to a complex text. Instead, analyze the text in advance for the four elements of text complexity (see Figure 1.2) and choose one or two aspects to highlight through your modeling.

When Mr. Jefferson's first-grade class was reading *The Three Little Wolves and the Big Bad Pig* (Trivizas, 1993), he knew that his students would not have difficulty with prior knowledge as they had been comparing folktales for several weeks. He also knew that his students would not have trouble understanding the genre, organization, or narration. However, the vocabulary demand was higher, with individual words such as *croquet, sledgehammer, concrete,* and *battledore and shuttlecock* likely to cause his students some confusion. In addition, he knew that he would have to model his thinking about the density of the text—especially focus on the change in roles—and the importance of the illustrations in conveying meaning.

At one point while modeling the text, Mr. Jefferson said,

> I want to reread this part because I think I'm getting confused. I think that the traditional story is getting in the way. The pig is the bad guy in this story because he's the one huffing and puffing and trying to blow the house down.

Later in the text, Mr. Jefferson said,

> I'm not sure that I've ever heard the phrase *battledore and shuttlecock* before. When I look at the picture, I see the wolves playing a game that looks like tennis, but there isn't a ball. It reminds me of badminton. It's a strange little thing that they're hitting back and forth. That must be the game that they're playing because the author says that they are playing *battledore and shuttlecock* in the garden when they see the big bad pig.

Model Ways to Resolve Problems

The second principle of modeling is that you model ways to resolve problems and confusions. Complex text by definition is going to

challenge students' understanding across one or more of the four elements that contribute to the text complexity (see Figure 1.2). Modeling is an ideal time to show students how you get yourself going again when comprehension breaks down. Often, it is the vocabulary that interferes with understanding. It is impossible to try to directly teach all of the words students will encounter as they read. Instead, teachers must help students build habits related to word solving. As noted in the Common Core State Standards, students should learn how to use context clues, word parts or morphology, and resources to uncover the meaning of unknown words. These three categories are worthy of attention during modeling.

Structural Analysis: Looking Inside Words

When readers come to an unknown word, one of the things that they can do is look inside the word to see if there are any clues to the word's meaning. Understanding morphology, including prefixes, suffixes, roots, bases, and cognates, helps the reader make an educated guess about an unknown word. For example, if the reader has never been exposed to the word *paleozoology*, she or he can make an educated guess about this field using knowledge about prefixes and suffixes. In fact, the word is fairly easy to figure out when you remember that *paleo* means old or ancient, *zoo* relates to animals, and *-ology* relates to the study of something.

But simply providing students with a morphology list is not likely to change their behavior when they come to unknown words. Instead, teachers need to model the use of morphology in understanding words. For example, while reading a sentence that contained the word *heterozygous*, the biology teacher modeled his use of morphology saying, "I know that *hetero* means different, so this must be the one that has two different alleles, or different versions, of a specific gene."

Of course, morphology does not always work, and students should be provided with examples that remind them to check other clues as well. Our favorite example of this occurred in an English as a Second Language classroom when the teacher got to the word *repeat*. She said,

> I got this one. I know that *re-* means to do again. So I'm going to *peat* again. Wait, I have no idea what that means! I better check the context clues and look outside the word to see if I can figure this out.

Context Clues: Looking Outside Words

In addition to looking inside words, students have to be taught to look outside of words to figure out their meaning. This happens through an understanding of context clues. Although context clues are not infallible, they can be helpful. There are a number of different kinds of context clues, such as embedded synonyms, antonyms, direct definitions, and the use of punctuation. Again, students need to be taught how to use these tools. Modeling provides students with examples that can be built into habits.

Novice readers make the mistake of approaching all texts as equivalent, when they are not. In too many cases, when the text is challenging, they turn away and give up.

Video 2.2

An elementary teacher models word solving.
www.corwin.com/ rigorousreading

For example, when reading about the "supermoon" predicted for March 19, 2011, the teacher noted the word *fatalities* in the news report. There had been quite a bit of news coverage around the world that this astronomical event, which brought the Moon into close range of the Earth, would cause widespread flooding and earthquakes. She made the connection between *fatalities* in the beginning of the sentence and the use of "the number dead" later in the sentence. Another example occurred when the teacher modeled using punctuation, in this case a dependent clause that contained additional and specific information about a more difficult word. Just as we discussed with word parts, teachers should model when the use of context clues fail.

Again, the goal is for students to develop a habit that they can use independently when they come across unknown words. Like most of the systems we use when reading and trying to make meaning, they don't always work. When these two systems—word parts and context clues—fail, it's time to look further outside the word and use resources.

What you are really modeling are the habits of active readers when confronted with challenging text. You are modeling persistence and a willingness to stick with something more difficult because it's worth it.

Using Resources: Looking Further Outside Words

"When all else fails, look it up" is a common motto of teachers, and for good reason. When the systems we have for figuring out unknown words within a text do not help, it's time to turn our attention to the resources we have at our disposal. Once upon a time, that was limited to printed dictionaries and glossaries. Today, we have a plethora of resources at our fingertips because of the Internet. For example, the visual dictionary (http://visual.merriam-webster.com) is a great resource that students can be taught to use. The same holds for the many specialized dictionaries, such as the following:

- **Science:** http://www.thesciencedictionary.com
- **History:** http://www.babylon.com/define/52/History-Dictionary.html
- **Mathematics:** http://www.amathsdictionaryforkids.com
- **Art:** http://www.artlex.com
- **Sports and fitness**: http://dictionary.babylon.com/sports

As with word parts and context clues, teachers should model their use of resources such as these and model the appropriate ways to ask other people for help. This can be as simple as calling a friend on the classroom phone or texting someone for more information.

Modeling word solving should be integrated with other approaches to understanding the text, such as those based on comprehension strategies and on using text structures and text features. We are not suggesting that teachers focus only on modeling word solving, but rather that they include word solving in their shared readings and think-alouds so that students have access to examples of expert thinking about words. It is important to emphasize that teachers should model their thinking, selecting the content of the modeling to coincide with the aspects of the text that contribute to their complexity. This is one of the keys to accessing complex texts. Modeling is not random, "whatever comes to mind," but rather purposeful instruction focused on specific identified aspects of text complexity.

Model How You Interact With Text

A third principle of modeling provides students with examples of how proficient readers act on text to support their comprehension. Complex text requires interaction with the text, yet many students approach texts rather passively. They don't know that they should be making notes to themselves, especially to guide their rereading. Annotation of text, the practice of making notes for oneself during reading, is an essential practice for closely reading complex text. As well, it is useful when writing about the text, as students consult their annotations to formulate arguments, analyze information, and make connections within and outside of the text. Importantly, these annotations have a life beyond their initial construction. They are used in discussions, and some teachers even collect the annotated texts for the purpose of assessment. Adler and Van Doren (1972) describe the most common annotation marks:

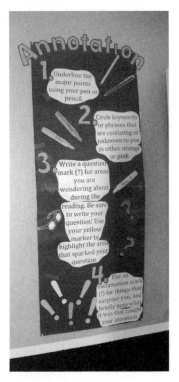

- **Underlining** for major points.
- **Vertical lines in the margin** to denote longer statements that are too long to be underlined.
- **Star, asterisk, or other doodad in the margin** to be used sparingly to emphasize the ten or dozen most important statements. You may want to fold a corner of each page where

Modeling is an ideal time to show students how you get yourself going again when comprehension breaks down.

you make such a mark or place a slip of paper between the pages.

- **Numbers in the margin** to indicate a sequence of points made by the author in development of an argument.
  - **Numbers of other pages in the margin** to indicate where else in the book the author makes the same points.
  - **Circling of key words or phrases** to serve much the same function as underlining.
- **Writing in the margin, or at the top or bottom of the page** to record questions (and perhaps answers) that a passage raises in your mind. (pp. 49–50)

These annotation methods are ideal for use during modeling, as they allow teachers to demonstrate the habits of an active reader. The types of annotations should be consistent with the developmental needs of students. For example, in the primary grades annotations are confined to underlining key points and circling unfamiliar words. As students progress into the intermediate grades, teachers begin to add other marks to indicate surprise or highlight questions we may have. In our modeling of annotations, we make sure that we are also writing our observations or queries so we can consult them later. As students move into middle and high school, we add numeration of the author's arguments and claims.

Student annotation can be limited when students can't write directly on the text. We circumvent this in several ways. Sometimes we ask students to annotate on sticky notes they affix to the page. If the passage is a shorter one, we photocopy it on large paper and ask them to write in the broad margins. Some of our colleagues have developed forms to accompany a reading, and one of our colleagues asks her students to slip the text into a clear plastic protective sleeve to develop temporary annotations.

As we noted earlier, modeling with complex texts teaches students the importance of persistence when confronted with challenge. Mere exhortations to try harder are insufficient; what is modeled should be a first step in equipping students with the tools they need to resolve comprehension problems. In the next section, we will discuss two methods for modeling with complex texts: think-alouds and shared reading.

Model Through Think-Alouds

The ninth-grade earth science class is focused on live video streamed from a news agency showing the eruption of a small volcano located near the Eyjafjallajoekull glacier in Iceland. The voice of the teacher narrates what he is seeing as he watches with his class. "As I'm watching this, I'm thinking about how unique this eruption is," he says. "With most volcanoes, there are earthquakes that signal something might be happening. But these volcanoes around Iceland don't give any warning. I checked on the USGS website, and the tremors were really small." He continues, "I'm also noticing that the eruption is more like a fissure. See how it's tearing here?" he gestures. "It's awfully close to this glacier. If the fissure keeps widening, it's going to have an impact on the glacier itself." The teacher concludes, "I know this area [in Iceland] is where the Eurasian and North American tectonic plates meet, because I looked on this map. I'm guessing that there's been significant movement of those plates, and this volcanic eruption is the result."

As noted in the Common Core State Standards, students should learn how to use context clues, word parts or morphology, and resources to uncover the meaning of unknown words.

Without the teacher's exposure of his thinking, his students would be left to their own devices to draw conclusions about the natural disaster they were witnessing. In a matter of two minutes, the teacher demonstrated how he used his background knowledge ("I'm thinking about how unique this eruption is"), consulted resources (the U.S. Geological Survey and a tectonic plate map), applied expert noticing ("See how it's tearing here?"), and speculated ("I'm guessing that there's been significant movement"). This teacher's use of a think-aloud procedure is a quality indicator of how expertise is shared in the classroom. Students deserve, at some point in the lesson, to experience the curriculum from the experts' perspective. This provides them with an opportunity to imitate the expert thinking, almost like an apprentice would in learning a new skill. Imitating is one of the ways humans learn, and modeling taps into this system (Fisher, Frey, & Lapp, 2008). Tips for effective think-alouds can be found in Figure 2.2.

Teachers regularly use modeling and demonstration to show students how a skill, strategy, or concept is used. While often associated more closely with performance tasks like swinging a tennis racket or playing a musical instrument, modeling is equally effective for cognitive and metacognitive tasks. Modeling includes naming the task or strategy, explaining when it is used, and applying analogies to link to new learning. The teacher then demonstrates the task or strategy, alerts learners about errors to avoid, and shows them how it is

Figure 2.2 Tips for Effective Think-Alouds

Choose a short piece of text. Think-alouds are often the most effective when they are focused and well paced. A brief think-aloud delivered using a passage of one to four paragraphs will have more impact because student interest will be maintained. As well, it will prevent the temptation to model too many strategies.

Let the text tell you what to do. Don't plan to go into a think-aloud cold, without having read the text, because your teaching points will be unfocused. Read the text several times and make notes about the comprehension strategies you are using to understand the text. These notes will provide you with ideas for the content of your think-aloud. Annotate the text so you will have something to refer to as you read.

Keep your think-alouds authentic. It can be a little disconcerting to say aloud what's going on in your head. Most teachers adopt a conversational tone that mirrors the informal language people use when they are thinking. An overly academic tone will sound contrived. It's better to say, "Hey—when I read this part about the penguins, right away I saw a penguin in my mind," rather than, "I was metacognitively aware and activated my visualizing strategy to formulate an image of a penguin as I read that paragraph."

Think like a scientist, mathematician, historian, artist, literary critic . . . Your shared reading texts are chosen because they have content value. Thinking aloud doesn't mean that everyone suddenly has to be a reading or English teacher. Make your think-alouds authentic by telling students how you process text through the lens of **your** content expertise. This elevates the think-aloud because you are showing them how your understanding of content text is influenced by what you know about the content.

Tell them what you did. Using an authentic voice doesn't mean you can't name the strategy. Tell your students what strategy you used to help you comprehend. This allows them to begin to form schemas about reading comprehension. Underline or highlight words or phrases that helped you understand and encourage students to do likewise, if possible.

Resist the urge to "over-think." The meaning of the passage should not be sacrificed for the sake of the think-aloud. Don't insert so many think-alouds into the reading that the intended message is lost. Fewer well-crafted think-alouds will have far more impact than a stream-of-consciousness rap that leaves the students bewildered by what just happened.

Source: Adapted from Fisher and Frey (2012b). Printed and electronically reproduced by permission of Pearson Education, Inc., Upper Saddle River, New Jersey.

applied to check for accuracy. Modeling is often accompanied by a think-aloud procedure (Davey, 1983) to further expose the decisions made by an expert as he or she processes information. For this reason, the think-aloud consistently contains "I" statements to invite the learner into the mind of the teacher.

In addition to looking inside words, students have to be taught to look outside of words to figure out their meaning.

This is a profound shift from what most teachers are accustomed to doing. Much of classroom instruction is in the second person and is interrogative in nature ("When you look at this eruption, what do you see?"). Teaching and quizzing become the order of the day, and students walk away from the class under the false assumption that somehow the teacher just "knows" the answer. They are not made privy to the speculative, at times hesitant, thinking of the content expert. What's lost are the natural stutter-steps made by someone who is deeply knowledgeable of the complexities of the topic.

It's understandable that many teachers struggle with making this a part of their instruction. The majority of instruction they have encountered has been the interrogative kind. They don't have an internalized monologue of what an effective think-aloud sounds like. Therefore, it's useful to introduce teachers to some quality indicators related to modeling and thinking aloud. We've found it particularly helpful for teachers to watch each other model and then talk about how it felt, both as the person modeling and the person observing expert thinking. Some of the indicators we look for during teacher modeling include

- naming a strategy, skill, or task;
- stating the purpose of the strategy, skill, or task;
- using "I" statements;
- demonstrating how the strategy, skill or task is used;
- alerting learners about errors to avoid; and
- assessing the usefulness of the strategy or skill.

Importantly, after receiving adequate time in scaffolded instructional support that includes modeling, the students should be able to complete tasks using the skill or strategy that was modeled for them. In other words, modeling provides students with examples, not a recipe, that they can follow as they complete their own work.

Model Through Interactive Shared Readings

Shared reading is an instructional procedure that uses appropriately complex text that can be viewed by both the teacher and the student at the same

time (Holdaway, 1979). The responsibility for reading the text is shared because the students follow the print silently while the teacher reads aloud. During subsequent rereadings, students can read aloud as well.

For younger students in kindergarten through second grade, an oversized version of a picture book measuring approximately 24 inches or more in width is commonly used. The primary advantage of using a big book is that the large print and illustrations are visible to the students. Teachers of older students often display the shared reading text on a document camera, or many provide each child with a copy to write on. In other cases, a reading from the basal or a textbook is used. At all times, the passage chosen should be one that is complex in regard to its structure, its levels of meaning or purpose, its use of language conventions, or its high knowledge demand.

The interactive nature of shared readings allows teachers to move beyond simply conveying text to elevating a lesson to focus on discourse. Students at all grade levels benefit immeasurably from discussion with peers. These lessons are not passive, and they provide students with many opportunities to develop their academic language through the use of verbal expressions of ideas. In addition, they require students to listen closely not only to the text being read but to the comments of their peers as well.

Characteristics of Interactive Shared Reading Lessons

Shared reading is recognizable in the way it is delivered by the teacher. A shared reading event is likely to be short and lively, and the text is read more than once to reinforce the skills or strategies being taught. It also helps students build the habit of rereading when the text is complex. As students become comfortable, they are encouraged to read along with the teacher. Rog (2001) describes five characteristics of shared reading:

- Uses large print
- Provides brief, engaging lessons that encourage student participation
- Suits mixed-ability groups
- Includes repeated readings to reinforce concepts
- Emphasizes skills at the letter, word, sentence, and text levels

A well-constructed interactive shared reading lesson serves as an effective method for introducing key strategies and skills through active teaching. Shared reading allows the teacher to instruct through modeling by demonstrating how a skill or strategy is applied to a reading. After modeling, the teacher asks questions to foster discussion and provides prompts to scaffold students' understanding as they read text that is initially new to them. Students interact with one another as well to support each other as they apply the new skill or strategy.

Again, the goal is for students to develop a habit that they can use independently.

Of course, it is essential to remember that the act of shared reading does not create readers—it is what the teacher does inside the shared reading event that makes the difference. Like all aspects of teaching, a successful shared reading lesson requires careful planning. Effective teachers

1. craft their lessons based on the needs of the students;
2. identify materials that furnish the features necessary for the teaching purpose; and
3. create a sequence of instruction that includes

   - modeling through demonstration,
   - scaffolding through questions and prompts, and
   - supporting through peer interactions.

In this way, students acquire important skills and strategies needed for accurate, efficient, and meaningful reading.

Pressley et al. (1992) observed a second-grade teacher use a think-aloud process during a shared reading of *Where the Wild Things Are* (Sendak, 1963). This text is complex in that it requires students to move back and forth between a realistic setting and a dreamlike one. The teacher used both visualization and prediction strategies to focus her students' attention on her anticipation of this shift:

> That night Max wore this wolf suit and made mischief of one kind and another . . . Boy, I can really visualize Max. He's in this monster suit and he is chasing after his dog with a fork in his hand. I think he is really starting to act crazy. I wonder what made Max act like that . . . Hm-m-m . . . I bet he was getting a little bored and wanted to go on an adventure. I think that is my prediction.

In a fifth-grade classroom, Ms. Fleck thought aloud during a shared reading to make her understanding of the opening paragraph of *Old Yeller*

(Gibson, 1956) explicit for students. Her modeling was designed to invite them into the book. The first paragraph of the book reads,

> We called him Old Yeller. The name had a sort of double meaning. One part meant that his short hair was dingy yellow, a color we called "yeller" in those days. The other meant that when he opened his head, the sound he let out came closer to being a yell than a bark. (p. 1)

Ms. Fleck's think-aloud demonstrated the way in which a reader activates his or her prior knowledge, summarizes information, and predicts future events in the text. She said to the class,

> I like the way the author tells us how this dog was named—he got his name from the color of his fur *and* because of the sounds he makes. I think that is a great way to pick a name for a dog. I bet both of those things—his color and his bark—will be important as we read the story. The author is probably telling us this to get us ready for really important things in the pages to come. I had a dog like that. He used to make the most awful sound when he tried to bark. We never thought to call him "yeller," but wow, what a sound he could make.

Thus far we have discussed the reasons for modeling and the methods for doing so. But modeling requires active participation from the learner as well. We can model all we want, and do it well, but some students will still miss the point if they don't clearly understand the purpose of the lesson. A purpose statement alerts the learner to what they should be attending to during your modeling, and how they will use it in their own learning. In the next section, we will examine the role of establishing purpose in order to ensure access to complex texts.

▶ Accessing Complex Text Requires a Clear Purpose

Each lesson should have a purpose, goal, or objective. As a profession, we teachers have known about the importance

Teachers should model their use of resources and model the appropriate ways to ask other people for help.

E.L.D.

Content Objective:
I know that my ideas may be spoken as a sentence.

Language Objective:
I can speak and write my ideas in complete sentences.

of purpose for several decades (Hunter, 1976). A clearly articulated purpose focuses instruction, provides students with an answer to the question "why do we have to learn this?" and allows for assessment of outcomes. It is a vital component for accessing complex texts, because it alerts students to what they should attend to as you model. In addition, it prepares them for the ways they will use the modeled information later in the lesson. Yet establishing purpose is a teaching behavior that is often neglected. In too many classrooms, students are left to intuit the purpose of a lesson. Simply said, establishing the purpose of the lesson facilitates student achievement (Marzano, 2009).

Teachers should model their thinking, selecting the content of the modeling to coincide with the aspects of the text that contribute to their complexity.

But what does a good purpose statement look like? It's more than simply stating the standard to students. A quality purpose statement provides information for students about what they will learn and how they might demonstrate that understanding. A quality purpose statement also helps the teacher plan the lesson, as the tasks students are asked to complete should align with the expected understanding. This is an important point that is easy to overlook. The purpose drives instruction, differentiation, and assessment. It might seem like an insignificant component of quality teaching, given that it should occupy only a fraction of the lesson, but we think it's the foundation of quality lesson planning and instructional delivery.

In our work, we use *purpose*, rather than *goal* or *objective*, because it forces us to pay attention to what the students think. Teachers write objectives, but students have to get the purpose. While teachers want objectives that are measurable, students want to know what they're expected to learn and why. We ask our students, "What are you learning?" rather than "What are you doing?" because we want them to notice their learning. That's why an agenda or lesson plan alone won't do. It is a list of tasks, but it doesn't address the purpose of learning.

Video 2.4

A collection of purpose statements in elementary classrooms.
www.corwin.com/ rigorousreading

Components of the Purpose Statement

There are a number of ways to think about components of a purpose statement. To be clear, the purpose statement should not focus on the tasks that students will complete as part of the class session or at home. Rather, the purpose statement should reflect the understandings that students will gain as a result of their engagement in the lesson components. When lessons are planned with the end in mind, purpose statements are easier to develop (Wiggins & McTighe, 2005).

Content

Part of the purpose statement comes from the content standards. This is, in part, why a clearly established purpose is critical. Planning an amazing lesson for ninth graders based on seventh-grade standards will not ensure that the students reach high levels of achievement. Having a purpose statement based on content standards ensures that instruction is aligned with high expectations.

Suggesting that the purpose is based on the content standards does not mean that the purpose *is* the standard. Most content standards take time to master. The purpose statement should focus on the learning for the day. For example, it takes weeks for students to understand the causes and impact of World War II, so several purpose statements that add up to this larger picture will be required. When standards are not analyzed for their component parts and instead are used as the purpose, students stop paying attention to them. The standards might be posted on the wall, but they're like wallpaper to students: a decoration that really doesn't have anything to do with today's work. An appropriate content purpose for second graders might be to "use information gained from the illustrations to understand the setting." This is an important part of their eventual understanding of reading anchor standard 7, but not the whole standard, as that will take much longer to accomplish.

Language

A second component of the purpose statement relates to the ways in which students can demonstrate their understanding of the content. This is often referred to as the *language purpose*, as humans demonstrate their understanding by reading, writing, speaking, listening, and viewing. Understanding the linguistic demands of the content is critical for this component of the purpose, which is especially valuable for English learners who are doing double the work, learning content and language simultaneously (Fisher, Frey, & Rothenberg, 2008).

To develop the language component of the purpose statement, teachers should consider the following:

- Vocabulary
- Language structure
- Language function

For some lessons, the important linguistic component might be related to the *vocabulary* of the discipline. For example, in second grade, part of the

Video 2.5

A collection of purpose statements in secondary classrooms.
www.corwin.com/ rigorousreading

Complex text requires interaction with the text, yet many students approach texts rather passively.

purpose might be for students to *use the terms time, place or location, or action when describing the setting.*

For other lessons, students need to focus on *language structure*—grammar, syntax, or signal words. For example, students learning the art of sourcing ideas might use a sentence frame, *While _____ believed _____, others disagreed* as part of their conversations with peers.

A third way to think about the language component is by determining the *function of language* that is necessary to understand the content. In other words, do students need to justify, persuade, inform, entertain, debate, or hypothesize to understand the lesson? For example, in a discussion about a particular text, part of the purpose might be to *justify your answer with evidence from the text.*

Annotation of text, the practice of making notes for oneself during reading, is an essential practice for closely reading complex text.

Communicate the Purpose Statement

Once a purpose statement has been constructed, it has to be communicated to students. There are a number of ways that teachers do this. Some post the purpose on the board and briefly talk about the purpose and its relevance for students at the start of the period. Others begin with inquiry and then invite students to talk about why they are doing what they're doing before making the purpose more explicit. And still others verbally discuss the purpose and then invite students to write the purpose in their own words as part of their note-taking tasks.

Regardless of how the purpose is established, it's important that students know the purpose of the lesson. It tells them what to pay attention to and what will be expected of them as they learn to access complex texts. A clearly communicated purpose increases the relevance of the lesson for students and helps the teacher remain focused on the lesson at hand without drifting too far afield and wasting valuable instructional time. In fact, this is the most common thing that teachers who begin establishing purpose tell us, "It really helped me stay focused." When asked about the impact of staying focused, we regularly hear "my students learn more" and "I have more than enough time to cover the standards, and cover them well." During the course of the lesson, unanticipated student misunderstandings may be revealed, and may necessitate deviation from the original instructional plan. However, even in these cases the purpose is valuable, as it helps the teacher and the students return once again to the intended focus of the lesson.

Video 2.6

Making sure students know the purpose.
www.corwin.com/ rigorousreading

▶ Summary

Mere exhortations to try harder are insufficient; what is modeled should be a first step in equipping students with the tools they need to resolve comprehension problems.

The first access point for students to engage with complex texts is established through modeling and setting the purpose. Modeling and thinking aloud provide your students with a glimpse of your cognitive and metacognitive processes as you read, understand, and interact with a text. They also alert students to the fact that as an expert reader, you know you have to activate additional resources in order to make sense of the text. For that reason, it is helpful to identify in advance the elements of a text that you believe will give your students more difficulty. After all, they really don't need you to model what they already know how to do. Make sure that students witness how you solve comprehension problems and annotate the text to support subsequent readings. These efforts are likely to be wasted if students don't know what they are watching and listening for, or if they are unclear on how they will apply it. Clear purpose statements that address the content and language demands of the lesson also assist students in focusing their attention.

Access Point Two

Close and Scaffolded Reading Instruction

M iddle school English teacher Armando Perez invites his students to read a short story called "Eleven" by Sandra Cisneros (1991). He points out to them that they are still exploring the inner lives of characters and considering how those lives compare to their outward lives—the ones that others can see. The students read the text independently, making notes as they go. Fernando underlines several sections in the text and circles two. Following their independent reading, Mr. Perez reads the text aloud to students, pausing to think aloud in the three places that seemed to have caused them confusion. He is able to pinpoint these particular sections of the text because he walked around the classroom observing his students as they made their annotations. He could thus target his modeling on these areas of confusion.

At one point, he pauses his read-aloud and says,

> They have a lot of years and numbers in this text, but
> this says that the sweater is maybe 1,000 years old. I'm

having a hard time believing that. I'm thinking that if it really were 1,000 years old, it would be in a museum. I'm thinking that this is an example of hyperbole that is being used to make a point.

Following his modeling, Mr. Perez asks his students to talk about a couple of questions, including "How is age like an onion, at least according to the author?" and "Why does she start crying when she has to wear the sweater?" The students talk with each other about these questions, often referring back to the text to locate specific information that they want to use in their responses.

Next, Mr. Perez asks students to talk with their team about Rachel's inner life, saying, "From what the author tells us, what can we surmise is going on inside Rachel's head when her teacher says that the sweater has to belong to someone?" The students focus on the words that the character Rachel uses to describe herself, such as "skinny," and on how the author refers to her "little voice." Jeremy says, "I don't think that Rachel has confidence because she stumbles on her answer to the teacher, and then it says that she's feeling like she is three again."

The Common Core State Standards have drawn increased attention to an instructional routine called close reading, known in some circles as analytic reading.

Mr. Perez continues inviting students to provide their arguments, with evidence, as they reread the text looking for examples. They talk with their groups often, and periodically are invited to share with the whole class. After having read the text at least four times, Mr. Perez asks his students to use their annotations to describe the inner life of one of the characters in the short story. He says, "You might select Rachel, but alternatively you could select Mrs. Price or Sylvia or even Phyllis. Just remember to describe the character's inner life using evidence provided from the text." As the students get to work, Mr. Perez meets with several who have struggled with tasks like this in the past, making sure that they are starting on the right track.

There are many different ways to engage students in reading. There are instructional routines that require extensive teacher support, such as shared readings, which are described in the previous chapters, and instructional routines that require extensive peer support, such as reciprocal teaching or literature circles, which are included in the next chapter. The Common Core State Standards have drawn increased attention to an instructional routine called *close reading*, known in some circles as *analytic reading*.

Figure 3.1   Comparing Close and Scaffolded Reading Instruction

	Close Reading Instruction	Scaffolded Reading Instruction
Grouping	Large or small group; heterogeneous	Small, needs-based; homogeneous
Text Difficulty	Challenging, complex grade-level texts	Challenging but tailored to the instructional needs of the group
Teacher Supports	Text-dependent questions; annotation; repeated readings	Questions to check for understanding, prompts for cognitive or metacognitive work, cues to shift attention, and direct explanations as needed
Purpose	Expose students to content that stretches their thinking and reading skills	Advance student reading skill levels; practice comprehension strategies; uncover and address errors and misconceptions

In addition, scaffolded reading instruction in small groups is useful in providing students access to complex texts. A comparison between close and scaffolded instruction can be found in Figure 3.1.

▶ Accessing Complex Text Requires Close Reading

Close reading is not a new instructional routine; in fact, it has existed for many decades as the practice of reading a text for a level of detail not typically sought after in everyday reading (Richards, 1929). Close readings should be done with texts that are worthy and that are complex enough to warrant repeated reading and detailed investigation. As Newkirk (2010) noted, not all texts demand this level of attention. But some texts do.

In those cases, the reader has to develop a fairly sophisticated understanding of what the author actually said. A problem, as described by advocates for close reading, is that students are often encouraged to answer questions that take them away from the reading prematurely and lead them to thinking about their own experiences. Instead, as Rosenblatt (1938/1995)

Video 3.1

Close reading with sixth-grade English language learners.
www.corwin.com/ rigorousreading

recommended, there must be a transaction between the reader and the text. Readers should develop an understanding of the author's words and bring their own experiences, beliefs, and ideas to bear on the text. In her words, "The reader must remain faithful to the author's text and must be alert to the potential clues concerning character and motive" (p. 11). Rosenblatt cautioned that readers might ignore elements in a text and fail to realize that they are "imputing to the author views unjustified by the text" (p. 11).

If students already knew how to do this, we would not be spending time focused on close reading. The problem is that students do not arrive already knowing how to interrogate a text and dig down into its deeper meaning. Teachers have to teach students how to do this, in both informational and literary texts. In other words, close readings are not exclusively for English teachers; close readings should be conducted in any class in which complex texts play a role, whether in science, social studies, auto mechanics, art, or physical education. Whatever the content may be, close readings of that content will always require the teacher to keep several important considerations in mind: the length of the selected text, the amount of time allocated for students to reread the text, the need to limit the frontloading of information when introducing the text, and the goal of having students annotate the text, ask text-dependent questions, and engage in text-dependent after-reading activities.

In the following section, we will describe in detail six close reading practices that guide students' understanding of complex texts:

1. Short, worthy passages
2. Students rereading
3. Limited frontloading
4. Text-dependent questions
5. Annotation
6. After-reading tasks

Short, Worthy Passages

Because close readings can be time consuming, it is often best to select shorter pieces of text for instruction. These selections, typically between three and nine paragraphs in length, allow students to practice the analytic skills required of sophisticated readers. Longer, extended texts are also used to encourage students to practice the skills that they have been taught during close readings. Close reading instruction is not limited to stand-alone short texts such as news articles, poems, or short stories. Close readings can be done with short passages from longer texts, especially when a section is especially challenging and is pivotal for understanding the larger message of the text. Of course, this requires that the teacher analyze the text for its complexity and determine which parts require close reading. Close reading is predicated of the notion that the text is well known to the teacher and deeply understood. This can be challenging for teachers of younger students, who might be tempted to view these passages rather simply and not mine them for their more complex elements.

Close readings should be done with texts that are worthy and that are complex enough to warrant repeated reading and detailed investigation.

Students' Rereading

As part of a close reading, students must read and reread the selected text several times. This requires that students have expanding purposes for each repeated reading. These rereadings can be completed independently, with peers, with teacher think-alouds, or any combination thereof. As noted in the example from Mr. Perez's classroom, complex texts do not give up their meaning easily or quickly. In addition to improving fluency, repeated readings contribute to the comprehension and retention of information (Millis & King, 2001) as well as enjoyment (Faust & Glenzer, 2000). The practice of rereading carries into adult life, as noted by Smith (2000), who found that to be one of the most common strategies adults use to understand text. Of course, there are a number of ways to facilitate students' rereading of the same text. Unfortunately, most readers do not like to reread things a second or third time unless there is a specific reason for doing so. During close readings, the purpose for each reading is made clear, and often, those purposes are related to looking for evidence in response to a specific question. Importantly, rereading also reduces the need for extensive frontloading.

Limited Frontloading

When students read a piece of text only one time, the teacher has to do lot of work to ensure their understanding. In other words, the teacher is doing the heavy lifting. When students read and reread a text multiple times and talk about the text with their peers, the teacher does not have to provide as much instructional support. The rereading, discussions, and text-dependent questions do some of this. During close readings, the teacher does not provide much in the way of pre-teaching or frontloading of content. The structure of the lesson itself is the scaffolding that was once delivered through frontloading.

As with inquiry, the goal of close reading is for students themselves to figure out what is confusing and to identify resources they can use to address their confusions. It is essential that they develop the metacognition needed to understand difficult texts. As with inquiry approach education (e.g., Donovan & Bransford, 2005), close reading is in part about discovering—in this case, discovering what the author meant and how to come to terms with the ideas in the text. For example, students were introduced to George Washington's "Farewell Address" in their humanities class. Consistent with a close reading approach, students read and discussed this text several times, over several days, to fully develop their understanding of the text and what role it played, and continues to play, in history. Had their teacher provided a great deal of information in advance of this reading, students might have skipped the reading entirely and focused on what the teacher said.

Revealing the content of the reading in advance is different from stating the *purpose*. Purpose statements focus on the reasons for reading but do not provide the students with all the information about the reading. In the first lesson, the purpose was for students to identify Washington's reasons for leaving office after his first term as president. However, he withheld the details of the content of the passage itself. In addition, had the teacher told students what to think about the text (a common problem with extensive pre-teaching), the investigative aspect would have been lost, and students would not have developed the thinking skills that they needed when encountering complex texts on their own. Through multiple readings, students were eventually able to identify the influential nature of the document on the Federalist Party development.

Close reading does not apply solely to informational texts. Consider the difference in the amount of student learning that would likely occur in following two scenarios: first, in a situation where students are told about the author's life, his reason for writing, and the historical significance of a sonnet such as "The Long Love" by Sir Thomas Wyatt; second, in a case where students are given a chance to encounter the text and struggle with the meaning. In the former, students are often told what to think, whereas in the latter, students are guided in their discovery. In an eleventh-grade British literature class, as this poem was discussed, one student said to another,

> The lines in this poem that stand out to me are "And in mine heart doth keep his residence," and "And therein campeth, spreading his banner." These lines stand out to me because they both are examples of how Wyatt uses love as a person, not just a feeling. Using the word "his" to refer to love as someone that is within him. It's like he's possessed with love.

Students do not arrive already knowing how to interrogate a text and dig down into its deeper meaning. Teachers have to teach students how to do this.

Later in their discussion, the students were asked to consider the extended metaphors in the poem. They had experience analyzing the metaphors in the text, understood what they were being tasked with, and were able to apply this knowledge to the poem. Another student responded,

> The major metaphor of the poem, I feel, is consistent because Wyatt talks about love as a thing living within him, within his heart and throughout the poem that does not change. At the end he even says, "But in the field with him to live or die?" Wyatt refers to love as his master and will follow him into the field.

The archaic language of the poem made this more complex, and it would have been tempting to teach students about the meaning of the poem in advance of their readings. But by allowing students to wrestle with, and ultimately discover, that the poet was writing about the all-consuming power of romantic love to turn a life upside down, these students were able to locate the poem's meaning for themselves. Grounded in the text, they are now ready to extend their thinking about connections to themes in literature and in their own experiences. Too much frontloading, in this case, might have prevented this learning. However, the students didn't come to these understandings simply through rereadings and through their teacher's practice of limited frontloading. Their teacher relied on text-dependent

Video 3.4

Close reading
and text-
dependent
questions in
upper elementary
school.
*www.corwin.com/
rigorousreading*

*Close readings
are not exclusively
for English teachers;
close readings
should be conducted
in any class in
which complex
texts play a role.*

questions to provide students with expanding purposes for rereading, and to guide their thinking.

Text-Dependent Questions

As part of every close reading, students should respond to text-dependent questions that require them to provide evidence from the text rather than solely from their own experiences. For example, if a British literature teacher asked students the personal question, "Have you ever been in love?" he would have derailed the class discussion before it even began. Most of us can imagine the chaos that would have ensued as a roomful of 17-year-olds gleefully chomped down on this question. However, a commitment to fully understanding the text will still lead students to find answers to these sorts of questions as they begin to see themselves and the world within the words of another (you couldn't prevent them from making these connections even if you tried!).

The types of questions students are asked influence how they read a text. If students are asked only recall and recitation questions, they learn to read for that type of information. If they are asked questions that require them to analyze, synthesize, and evaluate, they learn to read more closely and actively engage with the text. Unfortunately, many of the questions that students are asked are about personal connections, which may not even require them to have read the text at all. The architects of the Common Core State Standards in English language arts are challenging the practice of asking students questions that can be answered without reading the text. Instead, they are pressing for questions that require students to locate evidence within the text. These text-dependent questions require a careful reading of the text such that students can produce evidence in their verbal or written responses. This is not to say that personal connections should be avoided at all costs. After all, readers naturally compare the information they are reading with their experiences. However, the argument for text-dependent questions asserts that discussions (and writing prompts) should focus on the text itself to build a strong foundation of knowledge. This purposefully built foundational knowledge can then be leveraged by learners to formulate opinions and make connections that are meaningful and informed.

As an example, consider the following two questions a teacher *could* ask of her students who have been studying an essay from *Last Call at the Oasis* (Weber, 2012) titled "A Way Forward? The Soft Path for Water" by Peter Gleick:

- Has your family made any changes to reduce water consumption?
- What are the differences between soft and hard paths to water management?

The first question can be answered without ever reading the essay. A conversation about the first question may be very animated and interesting, but it does not require that the students develop any level of understanding of the information presented by the author. If you were to observe this lesson, you might witness significant student engagement in a class discussion about the first question. But consider whether the actual text factored into the discussion or remained sitting on their desks unused. Accessing complex texts doesn't mean simply having them nearby—readers actually have to read them. Asking questions that require students to have read and understood the text is crucial. The first question about family water consumption habits is actually irrelevant within the context of this essay, which focuses on systemic water conservation methods. It is important that as teachers we know how to engage students, beyond simply asking them to tell a personal story. The content itself can and should be used to engage.

Close reading is predicated of the notion that the text is well known to the teacher and deeply understood.

There are several ways to structure questions such that students return to the text to find evidence for their responses. We caution that these questions should not focus solely on recall. The emphasis should be on getting students to use explicit and implicit information from the text to support their reasoning. There are at least six categories of text-dependent questions that can be drawn from and structured into a progression that will move students from understanding explicit meaning to understanding implicit meaning, and from working at the sentence level to working across an entire text and even with multiple texts. As well, some of these question types may not be suitable for a particular reading; there is no requirement that all of these types need to be used with every piece of text. Figure 3.2 contains a graphic of these questions. Further, as students discuss a given text, they will likely cover many of the questions that could have been asked. When they do so, the teacher does not need to ask a prepared question. We like to think of the prepared text-dependent questions as a resource that the teacher has to scaffold students' understanding and hope that much of the classroom conversation addresses the content of the question. The question samples below are based on the water essay referenced above. Examples of text-dependent questions for texts at the elementary grade levels can be found in Figure 3.3.

Figure 3.2 Text-Dependent Questions

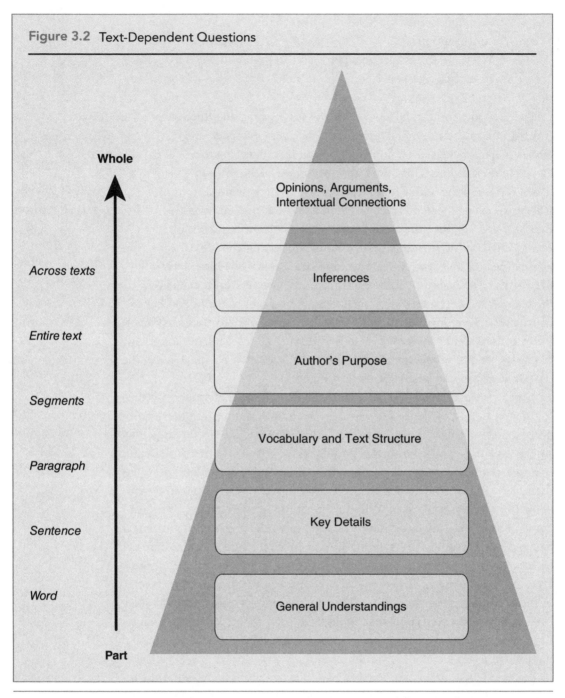

Source: Fisher and Frey (2013b). Used with permission. From *Common Core English Language Arts in a PLC at Work* by Douglas Fisher and Nancy Frey. Copyright 2013 by Solution Tree Press, 555 North Morton Street, Bloomington, IN 47407, 800.733.6786, solution-tree.com. All rights reserved.

Figure 3.3   Sample Text-Dependent Questions

Question Type	Questions From *Frog and Toad Together* (Lobel, 1971) in First Grade	Questions From Chapter 10 in *A Night to Remember* (Lord, 1955) in Sixth Grade
General Understandings	Retell the story using *first, next, then,* and *finally.*	Why would the author title the chapter "Go Away"?
Key Details	What ways did they try to solve the problem of eating too many cookies?	What are two things that could have prevented this tragedy?
Vocabulary and Text Structure	How did the author help us to understand what *willpower* means?	How does the chronological structure help the reader understand the events?
Author's Purpose	Who tells the story?	Whose story is most represented and whose story is underrepresented?
Inferences	Do you think Toad's actions caused the seeds to grow? Why?	Why would Mrs. Brown run lifeboat number 6 with a revolver?
Opinions, Arguments, Intertextual Connections	In your opinion, is Frog a good friend to Toad? Do you think this is a happy story or a sad one?	Compare this book with *Inside the Titanic* (Brewster & Marschall, 1997). What are the similarities and differences?

Source: Fisher and Frey (2012a).

General Understandings

These questions get at the gist of the text. What does the author want us to know or understand from the text? Often, these questions focus on the main claim and the evidence used to support the claim or the arc of the story or the sequence of information. For the water essay, the teacher might ask,

> "Which is the water path recommended by Gleick?"

Interestingly, this question is not directly addressed in the essay, and students will have to find clues from across the text to figure out his main claim. Alternatively, the teacher might direct students in this way:

> "Discuss the ages of water and why Gleick believes we are headed into the third age."

As implied in the structure of this directive, text-dependent work does not need to take place solely in a whole-class setting. Students can be encouraged to discuss their thinking with their peers. This particular exercise will lead students to a more clear-cut answer, but the act of engaging in the discussion is central to getting them to understand the essay and the key point that the author is trying to make.

Key Details

These questions focus on asking students about the important details that the author uses to inform the reader. Often these questions include who, what, where, when, why, or how in the stem. They can also include reference to the more nuanced details that must be understood to add clarity to the reading. For example, the following question is key to understanding Gleick's perspective:

> "What is the difference between water and water services?"

The teacher might also ask this:

> "What is one method Gleick identifies for reducing water consumption?"

Most readers do not like to reread things a second or third time unless there is a specific reason for doing so.

Key detail questions tend to focus on information presented directly in the text. Importantly, understanding this information should be critical to understanding the text; key detail questions should not focus simply on trivia. As well, these key details should be used to scaffold students' understanding as they respond to more complex questions.

Vocabulary and Text Structure

Some of the questions that students must consider revolve around the vocabulary used by the author, as well as the structure of the text itself. Text structure questions require that students consider the organization of the reading, such as the use of problem/solution or character dialogue to propel action. In asking questions related to vocabulary, teachers must be sure to make reference to both denotations (definitions) and connotations (the ideas or feelings that a word invokes) of words. In addition, as appropriate, the questions may focus on shades of meaning, word choice, figurative language, idioms, and confusing words or phrases. Finally, questions can provide students an opportunity to use context or structural clues to determine the meaning of unknown words. For example, the teacher might ask students about the three key ideas discussed in the essay about water:

> "After reading this essay, how would you summarize the differences between productivity, efficiency, and supply?"

When students read and reread a text multiple times and talk about the text with their peers, the teacher does not have to provide as much instructional support.

Alternatively, the teacher might ask students to determine the meaning of the word *ozonation* from the context clues or to discuss why the author chose the word emerged when talking about *Homo sapiens* over time. In addition, the teacher might ask students to comment on the structure of the essay and to note the differences between the parts in terms of tone and structure. Attentive students would notice those sections of the text with significant descriptions, with a reliance on problem/solution structures, and with a persuasive tone.

Author's Purpose

The genre of the text and the use of narration help students make sense of what they are reading. On the flip side, understanding the overall purpose of the text guides students in following the flow of the reading. Readers should understand if the text is meant to inform, entertain, persuade, or explain something to them. There are also situations in which the text has a specific bias or provides only part of the story. In these situations, students could be asked about the perspectives not explored in the text. For the water essay, some examples of questions related to the author's purpose are as follows:

"How does Gleick attempt to convince readers that water is a worthy issue of discussion?"

"What is Gleick's purpose in writing this? Is he trying to inform, entertain, or persuade? How do you know?"

"Is Gleick biased? What is your evidence?"

"Does Gleick acknowledge other perspectives? If so, what is the effect? If not, how does that influence your reaction to the piece?"

Inferences

Some of the questions that students need to think about require that they understand how the parts of a text build to a whole. Unlike the cognitive processes associated with inference at the local level, these inferences require students to consider the piece as a whole. They probe each argument in persuasive text, each idea in informational text, or each key detail in literary text, and anchor them to the central themes of the piece. Importantly, inference questions require that students have read the entire selection so that they know where the text is going and how they can reconsider key points in the text as contributing elements of the whole. In the Gleick essay, students might be asked questions like these:

Close reading is in part about discovering—in this case, discovering what the author meant and how to come to terms with the ideas in the text.

"How does the information at the start of the essay, about the U.S. using less water today compared with 30 years ago, help Gleick make his argument for the third age of water?"

"How does Gleick use the six differences between hard and soft paths to build the case for water services?"

Opinions, Arguments, and Intertextual Connections

The final category of text-dependent questions should be used sparingly, and typically comes after students have read, and reread, a text several times to fully develop their understanding. Readers should have opinions about what they read, and they should be able to argue their perspective using evidence from the text and other texts, experiences, and beliefs that they hold. For example, while reading about water, the teacher might ask questions like these:

> "Did Gleick make a convincing argument about the ages of water?"
>
> "Is there sufficient evidence presented that a soft path is the appropriate direction?"
>
> "How do Gleick's recommendations compare with those presented in the essay 'In Our Lifetime: Deconstructing the Global Water Crisis and Securing Safe Water for All' by Gary White?" (Weber, 2012)

These questions often result in deep and engaging conversations, especially when students have read and understood the text. Over time and with practice, students will begin asking themselves and their peers these types of questions, and the teacher will not be the only one who poses questions for discussion.

Annotation

In the last chapter, we recommended modeling annotation as a way to teach students how to interact with the text and how to interrupt the passive reading experience that can leave many of them struggling to find the meaning of a complex piece of text. Readers with a passive stance expect that the information will wash over them, and when it does not, they throw in the towel. Marking up the text allows them to witness their own growing understanding, and it encourages them to put into words what they do not yet understand. Annotation occurs first during their first or

second pass at the text, but should also continue throughout subsequent discussion framed by text-dependent questions.

Close reading does not apply solely to informational texts.

For example, in an eighth-grade unit of study on adolescence, humanities teacher Paula Brown used several pieces of text that allowed her students to practice their annotation skills. She had previously modeled annotation with several other pieces of text, print and digital, and felt they were ready to begin using it themselves. As she told her students,

> Adolescence is a time when important decisions—some of them life changing—occur. It can be scary to think that some of the choices you make now can last a lifetime. In this unit of investigation, you will explore what a parent, a poet, and a psychologist have to say about making decisions that seem small at the time, but are big in hindsight. The purpose of this unit is to examine adolescent decision-making from three perspectives in order to locate central themes.

As part of this unit, students read and annotated an article titled "Psychologist Explains Teens' Risky Decision-Making Behavior" (Iowa State University, 2007). For example, a section of Javier's text was annotated in this way:

> Gerrard said that the initial risk-taking experience will influence an adolescent's intention to repeat the behavior in the future. They do consult their conscience over risk-taking, but not always in a classic "good vs. evil" way.
>
> "From a kid's perspective, if you're operating in this more reasoned, thoughtful [experienced] mode—then you have the proverbial devil and the angel over your shoulder," she said. "If you're operating in the more experiential [impulsive] mode, you don't even know the angel is there. Those things are not in your mind at all, and the devil's only saying, 'This could be interesting.'" *EX*

After their first couple of readings through the text, Ms. Brown engaged students in a discussion using text-dependent questions, which encourage them to reread, and to consult their annotations, to deeply comprehend the passage. As part of their discussion, Ms. Brown asked students to consider the following questions, requiring that they provide evidence from the text for their responses.

- **General Understandings:** *What is the main finding of Dr. Gerrard's research?*
- **Key Details:** *What role does image play?*
- **Vocabulary and Text Structure:** *How did you figure out what* impulsive *and* reasoned *mean?*
- **Author's Purpose:** *Why is this genre appropriate for the content? Who is the intended audience for this article?*
- **Inferences:** *How can you determine that this is a credible source?*
- **Opinions, Arguments, and Intertextual Connections:** *Let's compare this article to the first reading we did ("Who's Right?"). How does this informational article explain some of the conflict occurring between mother and daughter?*

Throughout the discussion, the teacher reminded her students to mark up their text because "we read with our eyes, our brains, our hearts, and our pencils." She stated that the action of annotation gives them a sense of ownership and influence over the text and lowers the sense of intimidation that some readers feel when confronted with a difficult reading: "I want you to know that a reading shouldn't ever boss you around. I want you to see evidence of your growing understanding of the text as we get further into the discussion."

As part of every close reading, students should respond to text-dependent questions that require them to provide evidence from the text rather than solely from their own experiences.

After-Reading Tasks

Rather than take students away from the text, post-reading activities should require them to return to the text. For example, students may write an argumentative piece in which they use evidence from the text. They may engage in a Socratic Seminar (see page 131) or debate a topic. After-reading tasks should help students consolidate the meaning of texts and deepen their comprehension far beyond what they would be able to accomplish on their own.

Having students create short written summaries of complex texts provides them with an opportunity to solidify their understanding and to develop a catalog of notes for comparing multiple pieces of text in the future. You will recall that Paula Brown's unit on adolescence included three pieces of text. She noted, "It's hard for them to make comparisons across documents when they don't have meaningful notes, so I often have them do some précis writing so they'll have useful writing to draw from later in the unit." Following their discussion on the article written by the psychologist, Ms. Brown asked her eighth-grade students to summarize their understanding of the text. She told her students, "Write a short summary of about 100 words that accurately summarizes the article. Be sure to include the name of the researcher and the findings. And remember to use your annotations to guide your writing."

Précis writings are summaries of a text or passage that require students to distill the main points but also involve them in the process of "selecting, rejecting, and paraphrasing ideas" (Bromley, 1985, p. 407). Teaching students how to compose précis writings develops their ability to understand the text more deeply and to learn essential content. These writing tasks do not contain the student's opinions or questions and should not include any information not discussed in the text itself. The students in Ms. Brown's class will later use these précis writings to produce a longer essay in which they address the topic of adolescent decision making from different perspectives.

Close readings are an important component of reading instruction, but they are not the only instructional routine that students need to experience to become successful readers. As literacy educators, you have to ensure that students are engaged in reading texts that are worthy of their time. You also have to ensure that students investigate the text sufficiently to really develop an appropriate level of understanding. Combined with shared, collaborative, and independent readings, close readings provide students the experiences they need to become skilled in analytic reading, a prerequisite for college and career success.

Close Reading for Young Readers

Thus far, the examples we have offered have involved older students, but if you are a primary teacher, you may be thinking, "How could this ever occur with my students?" K–3 students have an especially wide gap between the level of texts they can read on their own and those they can read with some adult support. In other words, they can understand narrative and informational texts that far outstrip their current reading levels. It is for this reason that the list of text exemplars in Appendix B on the Common Core State Standards document contains read-aloud examples for the primary grades. One example is the use of *The Wonderful Wizard of Oz* (Baum, 1900/2000) in kindergarten. No one would expect five-year-olds to read this book on their own, or even with adult support. Rather, the intention is to expose young

If students are asked only recall and recitation questions, they learn to read for that type of information.

Video 3.5

Close reading in the primary grades.
www.corwin.com/ rigorousreading

students to complex texts that challenge their thinking skills rather than their reading skills. Perhaps we should refer to this as *close listening*, because so much of this is about listening comprehension.

Read-alouds such as this should not be confused with the soothing after-lunch read-alouds teachers sometimes use. Being read aloud to plays an important role in reading for pleasure, and most of us have fond memories even decades later of read-aloud experiences such as this. We do not advocate that this practice be abandoned. However, we do advocate the addition of read-alouds that are designed to develop the critical thinking skills these students will use across their reading lives. We are referring to interactive read-alouds (Fisher, Flood, Lapp, & Frey, 2004) that require students to actively participate in the co-construction of knowledge and understanding in ways that are similar to the close readings described in the section above. Close listening (reading) lessons use an interactive think-aloud approach that draws from many of the same principles as those used for older students:

The architects of the Common Core State Standards in English language arts are challenging the practice of asking students questions that can be answered without reading the text.

- Uses short, worthy readings that are complex due to structure, use of language conventions, levels of meaning, or knowledge demand
- Requires the text to be reread several times throughout the lesson
- Frames discussion and deepens student understanding of the text through the use of text-dependent questions
- Relies on after-listening tasks that require students to draw on knowledge of the text

Kindergarten teacher Mohamed Hassan uses readings from Aesop's fables to promote close listening. "These short tales are great for my kids during the first few months of school," he said. "They challenge them to really listen closely to get the details." He cited "The Lion and the Mouse" as an example.

"The version I use has some tough vocabulary in it, like *gnawed*, and *plight*, and *bound*," he said. "Great general academic words." He continued, "So I give them an introduction, really just a reminder about what we already know about how these fables work, so we're always looking for the moral of the story." The story is less than 200 words long, and after reading it to them twice, he fosters a discussion using text-based questions:

- **General Understandings:** *What happened? Tell me the story using your own words.*

- **Key Details:** *How did the lion help the mouse? How did the mouse help the lion?*
- **Vocabulary and Text Structure:** *What does the mouse mean when he says, "Perhaps I might be able to do you a turn one of these days?"* (Mr. Hassan said that he rereads the story again to them after posing this question.)
- **Author's Purpose:** *What is the moral of the story that Aesop wants us to know?*
- **Inferences:** *Why is the lion so surprised at the idea that a mouse could help him? What does the lion say and do that helps you answer this question?*

This is not to say that personal connections should be avoided at all costs. After all, readers naturally compare the information they are reading with their experiences.

Mr. Hassan uses students' knowledge of the traditional telling of this tale, with its more difficult language structures, to introduce them to a wordless illustrated version of the story. "Sometimes I use an animation video with the sound turned off, and other times there is a print version available. Depends on the story," he added. In this case, he used Pinkney's (2009) *The Lion and the Mouse.* "Now they are retelling the story with each other using the illustrations, and it's amazing to hear them use more sophisticated language in their oral retellings because they know the original version so well," he said. "That use of oral language skills is so important in getting their reading off the ground."

While annotation isn't featured when using read-alouds, it can be a part of a shared reading experience that gives students visual exposure to the text. Poems on chart paper, projected readings, and texts that come in the form of big books all have a role in close reading in primary grade classrooms. Interactive SMART Boards have annotation features that are easily used by students, and low-tech items such as highlighting tape and reusable wax sticks work well in temporarily annotating large print items.

The first half of this chapter has been dedicated to close reading practices that guide students' understanding of complex texts. A key feature of this type of instruction is the use of text-dependent questions that draw students back into the reading. It's really the progression of the questions themselves that guides student thinking. But students are also developing their reading skills, and they need experiences with texts that are still complex but may not be as far up the proverbial staircase of complexity as the texts that are used in close reading. This needs-based practice, called *scaffolded reading instruction*, relies on questions, prompts, and cues to foster students' cognitive and metacognitive skills.

▶ Accessing Complex Text Requires Scaffolded Reading Instruction

In scaffolded reading instruction, small groups of students with similar learning needs are grouped together for a short time to receive specific instruction from the teacher using text that will require instruction and support. These materials may include leveled texts for students in the primary grades (K–2) and complex texts, textbooks, or other readings the teacher has gathered for students in grades 3 and beyond. The purpose of scaffolded reading instruction is to deliver customized lessons based on recent assessment information. These assessments may be collected during the scaffolded reading instruction lesson itself or at other times during the day.

Scaffolded reading instruction typically lasts between 10 and 20 minutes, depending on the needs and stamina of the students. Stamina is a legitimate consideration for scaffolded reading instruction because this intensive instructional time may be the most cognitively demanding time of the day for students. In secondary classrooms, where instructional periods are far shorter than the 120 minutes allocated in elementary classrooms for reading instruction, a teacher may meet with only one group each period. However, these meetings are not limited to students who struggle with reading. In fact, all students benefit from this responsive instructional arrangement that allows the teacher to provide scaffolds with precision when needed and to withhold them when they are not necessary.

In the following section, we will describe in more detail the principles and practices and that guide effective scaffolded reading instruction:

- The student, not the teacher, is the reader.
- Small groups help differentiate support.
- Students have similar strengths and needs.
- Grouping patterns change frequently.
- Using questions and providing prompts and cues guide learners.

We will also discuss why *whole-class* scaffolding reading instruction creates difficulties.

The Student, Not the Teacher, Is the Reader

Everything in a scaffolded reading instruction lesson is designed to lead to the student reading the text. Often, this is accomplished through silent reading. The teacher may designate stop points in the text so the group can discuss the reading and clarify misunderstandings. Not surprisingly, this is not realistic with emergent readers who do not read silently, or with early readers who are just beginning to do so. Therefore, it can be tempting to have each student take a turn and publicly read a portion of the text. This practice, called *round robin reading*, is an ineffective and potentially detrimental approach to reading instruction (Optiz & Rasinski, 2008).

Another practice, called *choral reading*, refers to the practice of having students read in unison. Choral reading can be an effective tool for building fluency through repeated readings, especially in reader's theater. It is also an appropriate strategy for dramatic performances such as the recitation of a poem. Its usefulness is limited in scaffolded reading instruction, however, because the purpose here is to provide more individualized support for students. There may be brief passages that lend themselves to choral reading, particularly alliterative sentences or rhyming passages that beg to be heard aloud. That said, the student-reading portion of the scaffolded reading instruction lesson should be devoted to the individual.

There are at least six categories of text-dependent questions that can be drawn from and structured into a progression that will move students from understanding explicit meaning to understanding implicit meaning.

Small Groups Help Differentiate Support

The purpose of holding scaffolded reading instruction groups to no more than six is to ensure that the teacher can provide more direct contact time with each learner. When group sizes grow beyond this number, management demands may take precedence over instruction. In addition, the small size of the group allows the teacher to observe each student up close in the act of learning. Insight into a learner's problem-solving skills can inform future instruction because the teacher gains an understanding of what the students do when they get to a "tricky part."

Although the group should not exceed six, it is acceptable for it to be as small as one student. This is especially true when working with students who struggle with reading. While it may be tempting to place all the lowest-achieving students in one group, it is likely that they require more individualized instruction than their grade-level peers because their skill profiles are more idiosyncratic. In our experience, normally progressing readers tend to have a great deal in common with one another, whereas those who struggle tend to be unique in their patterns of strength and areas of need.

As we will discuss in the next chapter, the students who are not with the teacher in scaffolded reading instruction can be collaborating with their peers or working independently. Scaffolded reading instruction should not result in hours of independent work for the rest of the class.

Video 3.6

Teacher working with groups of students to facilitate their understanding. *www.corwin.com/ rigorousreading*

Students Have Similar Strengths and Needs

Most commonly, teachers form scaffolded reading instruction groups based on similar literacy strengths and needs, called a *homogeneous group*. This is done for two reasons: practicality and peer support. It is practical because the teaching day simply does not have enough minutes in it to allow for individual instruction for each student. Small-group structures also capitalize on the power of peer influence on learning. Stated another way, students benefit from the questions and insights of their peers in a teacher-directed group.

Grouping Patterns Change Frequently

We have stated that students are grouped based on a number of considerations, especially student strengths and needs. It is also vital to remember that these grouping patterns should not be static. In other words, the scaffolded reading instruction group a child belongs to in September should not be composed of the same classmates in May. It is essential for students to benefit from numerous opportunities to learn with one another; flexible grouping patterns ensure this happens. It is equally critical that students see themselves as contributors to the learning of others; flexible grouping patterns ensure this happens as well. Of course, careful consideration about how students are grouped is only a small part of scaffolded reading instruction. These groups are formed to implement powerful forms of teaching in which questions, prompts, and cues are used to provide students access to complex texts.

Using Questions and Providing Prompts and Cues Guide Learners

Students need experiences with a range of complex texts—not just the ones highlighted for close reading, which are quite complex. During scaffolded reading instruction, teachers provide more support and guidance

Teacher using
prompts and
cues to guide
learning.
*www.corwin.com/
rigorousreading*

*Gist questions
focus on the main
claim and the
evidence used to
support that claim.*

Video 3.8

Teacher working
with small groups
of students
to generate
questions.
*www.corwin.com/
rigorousreading*

than they do during close reading. This requires a teacher who can listen carefully to what students are saying to give them just enough support to let them find the answer. At the heart of scaffolded reading instruction lies the strategic use of questions to check for understanding, prompts to trigger cognitive and metacognitive thinking, and cues as needed to shift attention more overtly (Fisher & Frey, 2010b). In other words, rather than relying on text-dependent questions and repeated reading for the scaffolds—as is the case in close reading—the teacher provides support by attending to the misconceptions and errors that students make. Scaffolded reading instruction also provides students with practice applying comprehension strategies while learning to resolve their confusions.

Questions to Check for Understanding

The subject of questioning is critical to scaffolded reading instruction because questioning is the very core of the instruction. Once students have finished the reading for the lesson, teachers should pose literal and inferential questions to them. Retelling is a query at the *literal* level and is closely associated with comprehension. Teachers should invite students to retell and encourage them to use their books to support their retelling. Readers should return to the text as needed, and this should be considered an acceptable classroom practice. For instance, asking how the Big Bad Wolf disguised himself in *Little Red Riding Hood* is an example of a literal question.

In addition, ask questions that require students to *infer* meaning about the text, such as questions that ask about the main idea, or about the author's purpose for writing the book. An example of an inferential question for the same book is inquiring about why the wolf chose to disguise himself as an old woman and not a young man. Questioning may also probe students' reactions and opinions of the text. Asking a reader about his or her thoughts concerning talking to strangers encourages students to form an opinion and to provide evidence for their responses. Although every question you may ask cannot be anticipated in advance, it is useful to prepare literal and inferential questions to begin meaningful discussion with students.

Scaffolded reading instruction begins when the teacher poses a question to check for understanding. This is not the time to assess students but rather a time to uncover misconceptions or errors. Students should be asked a variety of questions to check their understanding, and teachers should be continually on the lookout for misconceptions and errors.

For example, when Meghan Becovic asked a group of students to explain how they knew if something was living, she wanted to uncover their understanding of the scientific definition of life, a concept they had been reading about. When her students provided her with a number of correct responses, she changed direction asking, "So is evolution a characteristic of life?" When several students nodded positively, she knew that she had uncovered a misconception that she needed to address. There are a number of question types useful in checking for understanding, such as *clarifying* and *elaboration* questions in which students are encouraged to add details and examples to their answers. When students are asked to clarify or elaborate on their responses, misconceptions, errors, and partial understandings will reveal themselves.

Prompts for Cognitive or Metacognitive Work

When errors or misconceptions are identified, the first step in resolving them is to prompt the student to engage in mental work, either cognitive or metacognitive. Unfortunately, in too many classrooms, when errors are identified, teachers skip the prompts and cues and instead provide the missing information for students. In this case, the student has not done any of the work and likely did not learn anything from the exchange. Teachers can prompt students' background knowledge and experiences, the rules they have been taught, or the procedures commonly used to solve problems (Figure 3.4 contains a list of common prompts used during scaffolded reading instruction). For example, when Frank Acerno questioned his students about a science article they were reading, he uncovered a misconception about speed versus velocity. In prompting them, he asked, "Remember the animation we watched about driving to school? Velocity and speed have some things in common, but . . ." The students immediately responded with a quote from the animation, "velocity is speed with direction," and their misconception was resolved.

Key detail questions tend to focus on information presented directly in the text. Understanding this information should be critical to understanding the text; key detail questions should not focus simply on trivia.

Figure 3.4   Types of Prompts

Type of Prompt	Definition/When to Use	Examples
Background knowledge	Used when there is content that the student already knows, has been taught, or has experienced but has temporarily forgotten or is using incorrectly.	• As part of a science passage about the water cycle, the teacher asks, "What do you remember about states of matter?" • When reading about a trip to the zoo, the teacher asks, "Remember when we had a field trip to the zoo last month? Do you recall how we felt when it started to rain?"
Process or procedure	Used when established or generally agreed-on rules or guidelines are not being followed and a reminder will help resolve the error or misconception.	• The student is saying a word incorrectly, and the teacher says, "When two vowels go walking. . . ." • When the student has difficulty starting to develop a writing outline, the teacher says, "I'm thinking about the mnemonic we've used for organizing an explanatory article."
Reflective	Used to encourage students to be metacognitive and to think about their thinking, which can then be used to determine next steps or the solution to a problem.	• The student has just read something incorrectly, and the teacher asks, "Does that make sense? Really think about it." • When the student fails to include evidence in her writing, the teacher asks, "What are we learning today? What was our purpose?"
Heuristic	Used to help learners develop their own way to solve problems. These are informal problem-solving procedures. They do not have to be the same as others' heuristics, but they do need to work.	• When the student has difficulty explaining the relationships between characters in a text, the teacher says, "Maybe drawing a visual representation of the main character's connections to one another will help you." • When a student gets stuck and cannot think of what to write next, the teacher says, "Writers have a lot of different ways for getting unstuck. Some just write whatever comes to mind, others create a visual, others talk it out with a reader, and others take a break and walk around for a few minutes. Will any of those help you?"

Source: Adapted from Fisher and Frey (2013a).

Figure 3.5   Types of Cues

Type of Cue	Definition	Example
Visual	A range of graphic hints that guide students through thinking or understanding.	• Highlighting places on a text where students have made errors • Creating a graphic organizer to arrange content visually • Asking students to take a second look at a graphic or visual from a textbook
Verbal	Variations in speech used to draw attention to something specific or verbal attention getters that focuses students thinking.	• "This is important . . ." • "This is the tricky part. Be careful and be sure to . . ." • Repeating a student's statement using a questioning intonation • Changing volume or speed of speech for emphasis
Gestural	Teacher's body movements or motions used to draw attention to something that has been missed.	• Pointing to the word wall when a student is searching for the right word or the spelling of a word • Making a hand motion that has been taught in advance such as one used to indicate the importance of summarizing or predicting while reading • Placing thumbs around a key idea in a text that the student was missing
Environmental	Using the surroundings, and things in the surroundings, to influence students' understanding.	• Keeping environmental print current so that students can use it as a reference • Using magnetic letters or other manipulatives to guide student's thinking • Moving an object or person so that the orientation changes and guides thinking

Source: Adapted from Fisher and Frey (2013a).

Cues to Shift Attention

If prompts fail to resolve the error or misconception, teachers can assume a more directive role through the use of cues. Cues should shift students' attention to something they've missed or overlooked (Figure 3.5 contains a list of common cues used during scaffolded reading instruction). A simple cue might be, "Take a look at the figure on page 112. Does that help?" There are a number of cues that are effective, including gestural, verbal, visual, physical, environmental, and positional. Of course, teachers use these cues regularly in their initial teaching, but often fail to use them when students are stuck. While reading an article on migration during the U.S. westward expansion, Terri Goetz identified an error that was not resolved through prompting. She used her voice and a gesture to shift students' attention. While pointing to a graph, she said, "Population PER thousand," emphasizing the word *per* with her voice.

Readers should understand if the text is meant to inform, entertain, persuade, or explain something to them.

Direct Explanations

Sometimes, prompts and cues do not resolve the errors or misconceptions that students have. In those cases, students cannot be left hanging. Teachers must ensure that students have a successful learning experience, even if that means providing a direct explanation and giving the student the answer. Importantly, direct explanations should come after prompts and cues to increase the likelihood that students can connect this new information to a thinking process in which they were engaged. Following the direct explanation, the teacher should monitor students' understanding by asking them to repeat the information back in their own words or asking the original checking for understanding question again. In this way, students are accountable for the information and for processing the experience with their teacher.

The Trouble With Whole-Class Scaffolded Reading Instruction

The process we outlined above works best with small groups of students. It's a difficult process to put into place in a whole-class setting. While checking for understanding can be done effectively with the whole class, when the teacher moves to prompt or cue, some students disengage. Some students don't need the information that their teacher is providing right now, either because it's not relevant or because they already understand the concept. When some students disengage, they distract others.

Improving classroom management, however, won't improve this situation. Unless scaffolded reading instruction is done quickly and expertly and all of the students have a task to do while the teacher prompts and cues those who need it, some students will lose focus. It's just human nature. It's better to address misconceptions or errors with small groups of students or individually, especially while students work collaboratively or independently.

Inference questions require students to consider the piece as a whole.

Returning to the life science teacher, Meghan Becovic, and the students' misunderstanding of the definition of living, prompts and cues were used to ensure their eventual understanding. At one point, Ms. Becovic asked her students to identify the characteristics all living things share. Part of their conversation follows:

Jamal:	One thing for life is breathing.
Teacher:	Do all things breathe? Think about that.
Mubarik:	Yes. We have to breathe or die.
Teacher:	So, I'm thinking about plankton.
Anais:	No, some things don't breathe.
Mubarik:	Oh, yeah, I forgot. But there is a word for what I'm thinking.
Jamal:	Is it metabolism?
Mubarik:	Yeah, that's it. To be alive you have to have metabolism.
Anais:	Yeah, that was in the book. I remember now.
Teacher:	Is metabolism the same as evolution?
Jamal:	No, but living things have to evolve or die.
Anais:	Wait a minute. We said that before, that they will die.
Teacher:	Take a look on this page [pointing to a website displayed on a computer].
Mubarik:	It says that living things have to reproduce. It doesn't say nothing about evolution.
Jamal:	So, maybe things don't have to evolve to be alive. Maybe that's more long term, not if the thing is alive right now.

As their conversation continued, the students in this group reached greater understanding of the content because their teacher did not simply tell them the missing information but rather scaffolded their understanding through prompts and cues. We have to be sure we provide this type of support for students who are stuck. When this is not provided, students become dependent on adults for information. When this support is provided, students become independent thinkers and learners who thrive inside and outside of the classroom.

▶ Summary

Close reading and scaffolded reading instruction establish critical access points to complex texts because they begin the shift of responsibility to the learner. Through the process of close reading, students are learning to stay close to the text to gain knowledge. These close reading lessons can be done in whole-group or small-group settings, and it is the text itself that is the predominant source of information. But students are also acquiring the skills of reading, and they need practice in drawing on their own cognitive and metacognitive resources as they read. This is achieved through scaffolded reading and requires the teacher to offer supports that encourage students to use what they already know as well as what the text has to offer.

Access Point Three

Collaborative Conversations

Four sixth-grade students are deeply involved in a discussion about the book they are reading in their literature circle, *The Music of Dolphins* (Hesse, 1996). The story centers on a young girl who has been raised in warm Caribbean waters by a school of dolphins. Named Mila by her rescuers, she is brought to a facility to be studied by scientists who are interested in the language development of feral children. However, Mila hopes to escape this bewildering environment and return to the only family she has ever known.

David opens the conversation. "In chapter 53, Mila begs Doctor Beck to let her go back to the ocean, but the doctor says she can't because she will go to prison. What did all of you think about that?"

"I think Mila said it best on page 163—'I look at her. I am already in prison.' Mila feels trapped, like she's suffocating," offers Estefany.

Marisol holds up her notebook for everyone to see.

That sentence meant a lot to me, too. I drew a picture of a girl in a cage at the zoo as I read that. I was remembering her conversation with her friend Justin, when he asked her if she got tired of people coming to look at her all the time.

David asks another question when the group gets quiet. "Reynaldo, do you have an idea to add?" At this, Reynaldo responds,

> Well, I wrote this in my notebook: "Mila feels like she's just a thing, not a person, and that nobody except for Justin even tries to see her as anything more than a dolphin girl. It feels that way in school sometimes, when everyone is checking everyone else out and deciding whether they're cool or not. It's like no one even bothers to look past your clothes or hair or where you live."

Video 4.1

Teacher introduces literature circles. *www.corwin.com/ rigorousreading*

These students are participating in a collaborative learning format called *literature circles* (Daniels, 2002). In between meetings, they read independently and make notes in their notebooks to be used in the next discussion. Each meeting is moderated entirely by the students themselves, who determine the direction of the conversation and the next reading task. In this way, students collaborate with one another to access complex texts.

Collaborative learning is one of the critical linchpins through which students access complex text because it enables them to consolidate their understanding with peers and provide support for one another in the absence of the teacher. We use the term collaborative learning in reference to work done with peers. These peer-assisted learning opportunities furnish students with a means of applying the skills and strategies they have learned during modeling, close reading, or scaffolded instruction. Collaborative conversations are a vital facet of group learning.

▶ Accessing Complex Texts Requires Collaborative Conversations

Increasing the amount of time students talk using academic language has been a priority for decades (see Fisher, Frey, & Rothenberg, 2008, for a review). Simply said, students need practice with academic language if they are to become proficient in that language. We don't only mean in English class; students must learn to speak the language of science, history, mathematics, art, literature, and technical subjects if they are to become thinkers in those disciplines (Fang, 2012).

From the time that there have been educational standards, speaking and listening have been included. In other words, this is not new. What is new is the role that student-to-student interaction plays in the Common Core State Standards. Although there is a great deal of attention paid to the reading and writing standards, we believe that educators should also attend to the increased demands placed on the speaking and listening domain, especially in anchor standard number 1, which states that students should "[p]repare for and participate effectively in a range of conversations and collaborations with diverse partners, building on others' ideas and expressing their own clearly and persuasively" (Council of Chief State School Officers [CCSSO, 2010], p. 22).

There is much to note in this standard, which applies to students across the grade levels:

- First, students are expected to come prepared for the discussion. This has not been set forth as a priority in previous standards. More commonly, the work begins when students arrive and enter a group.
- Second, students are expected to collaborate with diverse partners. This will require changes in instructional routines and procedures. In essence, this standard sets the expectation that students should be able to engage effectively with a wide range of people, not just with their friends and others they choose to interact with. This expectation that students work with diverse partners is, of course, an expectation reflected in many workplaces, and one that seems worthy of pursuing through instructional efforts. Educators will need to be on the lookout for opportunities for students to interact with a wide range of peers.
- Third, students are expected to build on each others' ideas. This is also a marked difference as many

Video 4.2

Teaching students to collaborate.
www.corwin.com/ rigorousreading

Students need practice with academic language if they are to become proficient in that language.

students share their idea or understanding and then the conversation moves to the next person. Now students are expected to maintain the conversation and continually build on the ideas of others.

- Finally, they need to be able to do this as they express their ideas clearly and persuasively.

Anchor standard 1 in the speaking and listening domain of the Common Core State Standards presents increased expectations for students and is directly related to accessing complex texts. According to this standard, students have to discuss the complex texts they have been reading. Not only will this aid them in comprehending the text, but it will also provide them with practice in critical thinking, argumentation, and using evidence in their responses. The way this is operationalized in different grades is presented in Figure 4.1. We have bolded words and phrases that did not appear in the standards for the previous grade to highlight the instructional components for each grade. For example, students in ninth grade are expected to "summarize points of agreement and disagreement," which was not a stated requirement for eighth grade. This one change is significant, as most students are already skilled in summarizing points of agreement and are rarely asked to summarize the points of disagreement. Analyzing the differences in the standards by grade level, a practice known as *vertical alignment*, is critical if teachers are going to develop teaching points aligned with the standards.

For collaborative learning to work, teachers must structure the time students have to interact with their peers to work toward these new skills. We will limit our conversation about collaborative learning to those structures and habits that provide students increased access to complex texts. There are a host of collaborative learning routines that provide this type of access, and some that are useful in other ways. That said, it is important to recognize that students must be taught to collaborate with their peers.

Building Structures for Collaborative Learning

"I'm just not sure they're really doing anything of value when they're in groups."

This is perhaps the most frequent reservation we hear from educators when the subject of student collaboration comes up. Worried about the amount of instructional time dedicated to a group project, some teachers question whether it is better to simply tell students what they need to know. But telling alone isn't especially effective. Other teachers possess a fixed idea about the task itself, believing incorrectly that for the work to be worthwhile, it must extend over several class periods. Still others express concerns about individual students who prefer to work alone rather than in a group. Armed with these misgivings, many teachers list the benefits of group work, and then offer an apology: "It just doesn't work for the students I teach."

These apprehensions prevent otherwise innovative educators from deepening their instructional practices. And many of these qualms are rooted in the potential issues surrounding task complexity. Some teachers worry about logistic and behavior problems if the task is too easy or too difficult. They question the value of the learning itself, wondering aloud whether it's worth the fuss. And, at times, they may even question whether their students are capable of sustained group work without the constant presence of an adult. Addressing *task* complexity is key to ensuring that the time devoted to productive group work is in fact productive (Frey, Fisher, & Everlove, 2009). Quality indicators of appropriate task complexity take the following factors into account:

- Designs that require students to work together
- Structures that elevate academic language
- The presence of grade level work
- The opportunity for productive failure

Designs That Require Students to Work Together

Group tasks require the same sort of thoughtful design process that goes into other aspects of instruction. First and foremost, students need to know how to interact with one another and how to seek help. We have sometimes heard teachers remark that they shouldn't have to teach about the norms of interaction, as "students should know how to work with each other by now."

Video 4.3

Introducing partner talk.
www.corwin.com/ rigorousreading

The Common Core Standards anchor standard 1 sets the expectation that students should be able to engage effectively with a wide range of people, not just with their friends and others they choose to interact with.

Figure 4.1	Speaking and Listening Anchor Standard 1
SL.CCR.1	**CCR Speaking and Listening Anchor Standard 1:** Prepare for and participate effectively in a range of conversations and collaborations with diverse partners, building on others' ideas and expressing their own clearly **and persuasively.**
SL.K.1 Kindergarten Students:	Participate in collaborative conversations with diverse partners about **kindergarten** topics and texts with peers and adults in small and large groups. a. **Follow agreed-upon rules for discussion (e.g., listening to others and taking turns speaking about the topics and texts under discussion).** b. **Continue a conversation through multiple exchanges.**
SL.1.1 Grade 1 Students:	Participate in collaborative conversations with diverse partners about **grade 1** topics and texts with peers and adults in small and large groups. a. Follow agreed-upon rules for discussion (e.g., listening to others **with care, speaking one at a time** about the topics and texts under discussion.) b. **Build on others' talk in conversations by responding to the comments of others through multiple exchanges.** c. **Ask questions to clear up any confusion about the topics and texts under discussion.**
SL.2.1 Grade 2 Students:	Participate in collaborative conversations with diverse partners about **grade 2** topics and texts with peers and adults in small and large groups. a. Follow agreed-upon rules for discussion (e.g., **gaining the floor in respectful ways,** listening to others with care, speaking one at a time about the topics and texts under discussion.) b. Build on others' talk in conversations by **linking their comments to the remarks of others.** c. Ask for **clarification and further explanation as needed** about the topics and texts under discussion.
SL.3.1 Grade 3 Students:	Engage effectively in a range of collaborative discussions (one-on-one, in groups, and teacher-led) with diverse partners on **grade 3** topics and texts, **building on others' ideas and expressing their own clearly.** a. Come to discussions prepared, having read or studied required material; explicitly draw on that preparation and other information known about the topic to explore ideas under discussion. b. Follow agreed-upon rules for discussions (e.g., gaining the floor in respectful ways, listening to others with care, speaking one at a time about the topics and texts under discussion). c. Ask **questions to check understanding of information presented, stay on topic,** and link their comments to the remarks of others. d. **Explain their own ideas and understanding in light of the discussion.**

SL.4.1 **Grade 4 Students:**	Engage effectively in a range of collaborative discussions (one-on-one, in groups, and teacher-led) with diverse partners on **grade 4** topics and texts, building on others' ideas and expressing their own clearly. a. Come to discussions prepared, having read or studied required material; explicitly draw on that preparation and other information known about the topic to explore ideas under discussion. b. Follow agreed upon rules for discussions and **carry out assigned roles.** c. **Pose and respond to specific questions to clarify or follow upon information, and make comments that contribute to the discussion** and link to the remarks of others. d. **Review the key ideas expressed** and explain their own ideas and understanding in light of the discussion.
SL.5.1 **Grade 5 Students:**	Engage effectively in a range of collaborative discussions (one-on-one, in groups, and teacher-led) with diverse partners on **grade 5** topics and texts, building on others' ideas and expressing their own clearly. a. Come to discussions prepared, having read or studied required material; explicitly draw on that preparation and other information known about the topic to explore ideas under discussion. b. Follow agreed-upon rules for discussions and carry out assigned roles. c. Pose and respond to specific questions **by making comments that contribute to the discussion and elaborate on the remarks of others.** d. Review the key ideas expressed and **draw conclusions in light of information and knowledge gained from** the discussions.
SL.6.1 **Grade 6 Students:**	Engage effectively in a range of collaborative discussions (one-on-one, in groups, and teacher-led) with diverse partners on **grade 6** topics, texts, and **issues,** building on others' ideas and expressing their own clearly. a. Come to discussions prepared, having read or studied required material; explicitly draw on that preparation **by referring to evidence on the topic, text, or issue to probe and reflect on ideas** under discussion. b. Follow rules for **collegial discussions, set specific goals and deadlines, and define individual roles as needed.** c. Pose and respond to specific questions **with elaboration and detail** by making comments that contribute to the **topic, text, or issue** under discussion. d. Review the key ideas expressed and **demonstrate understanding of multiple perspectives through reflection and paraphrasing.**

(Continued)

(Continued)

SL.7.1 Grade 7 Students:	Engage effectively in a range of collaborative discussions (one-on-one, in groups, and teacher-led) with diverse partners on **grade 7** topics, texts, and issues, building on others' ideas and expressing their own clearly. a. Come to discussions prepared, having read or **researched material under study;** explicitly draw on that preparation by referring to evidence on the topic, text, or issue to **probe** and reflect on ideas under discussion. b. Follow rules for collegial discussions, **track progress toward** specific goals and deadlines, and define individual roles as needed. c. Pose **questions that elicit elaboration and respond to others' questions and comments with relevant observations and ideas that bring the discussion back on topic as needed.** d. Acknowledge new information expressed by others and, when warranted, **modify their own views.**
SL.8.1 Grade 8 Students:	Engage effectively in a range of collaborative discussions (one-on-one, in groups, and teacher-led) with diverse partners on **grade 8** topics, texts, and issues, building on others' ideas and expressing their own clearly. a. Come to discussions prepared, having read or researched material under study; explicitly draw on that preparation by referring to evidence on the topic, text, or issue to probe and reflect on ideas under discussion. b. Follow rules for collegial discussions and **decision making**, track progress toward specific goals and deadlines, and define individual roles as needed. c. Pose questions that **connect the ideas of several speakers** and respond to others' questions and comments with relevant **evidence**, observations, and ideas. d. Acknowledge new information expressed by others, and, when warranted, **qualify or justify** their own views in **light of the evidence presented.**
SL.9-10.1 Grade 9–10 Students:	Initiate and participate effectively in a range of collaborative discussions (one-on-one, in groups, and teacher-led) with diverse partners on **grades 9–10** topics, texts, and issues, building on others' ideas and expressing their own clearly and persuasively. a. Come to discussions prepared, having read and researched material under study: explicitly draw on that preparation by referring to evidence **from texts and other research** on the topic or issue **to stimulate a thoughtful, well-reasoned exchange of ideas.** b. **Work with peers to set rules** for collegial discussions and decision making (e.g., **informal consensus, taking votes on key issues, presentation of alternative views**), clear goals and deadlines, and individual roles as needed. c. **Propel conversations** by posing **and responding** to questions that **relate the current discussion to broader themes or larger ideas; actively incorporate others into the discussion; and clarify, verify, or challenge ideas and conclusions.**

	d. Respond thoughtfully to diverse perspectives, summarize points of agreement and disagreement, and, when warranted, qualify or justify their own views and understanding and make new connections in light of the evidence and reasoning presented.
SL.11-12.1 **Grade 11–12 Students:**	Initiate and participate effectively in a range of collaborative discussions (one-on-one, in groups, and teacher-led) with diverse partners on **grades 11–12** topics, texts, and issues, building on others' ideas and expressing their own clearly and persuasively. a. Come to discussions prepared, having read and researched material under study; explicitly draw on that preparation by referring to evidence from text and other research on the topic or issue to stimulate a thoughtful, well-reasoned exchange of ideas. b. Work with peers to **promote civil, democratic** discussions and decision making, set clear goals and deadlines, and individual roles as needed. c. Propel conversations by posing and responding to questions that **probe reasoning and evidence; ensure a hearing for a full range of positions on a topic or issue;** clarify, verify, or challenge ideas and conclusions; **and promote divergent and creative perspectives.** d. Respond thoughtfully to diverse perspectives; **synthesize comments, claims, and evidence made on all sides of an issue; resolve contradictions when possible; and determine what additional information or research is required to deepen the investigation or complete the task.**

This is true, but only to a point. While students may have ample experience with group work in previous grades, they don't yet know how to work *for you.* Therefore, we suggest that teachers post, teach, and revisit norms for interaction, especially those that explain how to debate and disagree without being disagreeable, and how to seek, offer, accept, and decline help graciously.

It is important that teachers keep task complexity in mind when introducing new routines to students. Students who are learning a new way to work with one another should not be challenged with demanding content at the same time. The task complexity itself should be temporarily lowered to make it possible for students to attend to the collaborative learning processes and procedures that are new to them.

Structures That Elevate Academic Language

Students also need to know how to use the academic language of the lesson. Students of any age or level of experience benefit from language scaffolds that encourage them to use academic language and vocabulary.

Video 4.4

Teacher outlining
expectations,
especially for
language usage.
*www.corwin.com/
rigorousreading*

The use of language frames (partially constructed statements and questions that frame original ideas) is highly effective during collaborative conversations. In particular, teachers may find that students need sentence starters as they get used to using argumentation in their discussions. These language frames can be posted on table tents or on chart paper. For example, Karen Jessop provided her students with the following frames when they wanted to offer a counter claim:

- I disagree with _____ because _____.
- The reason I believe _____ is _____.
- The facts that support my idea are _____.
- In my opinion _____.
- One difference between my idea and yours is _____.

Ensure Grade-Level Work

When students are engaged in productive group work, the expected level of rigor for a given task should be made clear. It really doesn't matter how good the instruction is if students in a fifth-grade class are working on third-grade-level content. The result is predictable—the students will have learned third-grade information, not fifth-grade information. Although we understand that there are students who currently perform below grade level, lowering expectations is not the way to close the achievement gap. Some students require scaffolded instruction, which involves the teacher using questions, prompts, cues, and direct explanations. As we noted in the previous chapter, students can be grouped based

on assessed needs, and the teacher can focus on those needs with small groups. Other students require supplemental or intensive intervention, which is the focus of the Response to Intervention efforts under way in most districts (Fisher & Frey, 2010a). Importantly, while students are working productively with their peers and have peer support and language brokers, they should be working on tasks and texts that facilitate their understanding of grade-level concepts. The texts that are used in collaborative conversations and peer learning should be suitably complex for where the students are within the school year. Keep in mind that the collective work of the group is to make meaning together, and, accordingly, the texts used can and should be more complex than those texts students have used in their independent reading.

Consider a task Mr. Bonine's life science students completed as part of their unit on energy in an ecosystem. Each group of students was provided an envelope that contained little slips of paper with words on them. The words on the slips of paper were terms for different organisms in an ecosystem. Students were asked to sort the words in any categorical system that made sense to them. As group members moved words into categories, they had to defend their placement to their peers. They were encouraged to use a language frame, "This organism, _____, belongs in the _____ category because _____." When Imani moved the paper with the word bacteria to a new column, she said, "This organism, bacteria, belongs in a new category because it doesn't fit in any of these others." Her team members agreed, putting their thumbs up to show their agreement.

Once students had their categories, Mr. Bonine introduced technical vocabulary, including the terms *autotroph* and *heterotroph*. He asked students to re-sort their organisms based on this new information. Spenser moved all of the words back to a pile, saying, "These categories of predator and prey don't work for this. This organism, zooplankton, belongs in the heterotroph category because it can't make organic compounds. Instead, it eats other organisms."

During the period, Mr. Bonine added additional terms, such as *decomposer* and *producer*, and asked his students to continue their sorts. In doing so, the students in this biology class completed tasks designed to ensure their learning of grade-level biology concepts. He then moved them into a complex reading on these concepts, a science piece on the use of heterotrophs for recycling and biodiesel production, and students met in small groups to discuss the article. And that's what collaborative learning should do: It should provide students with an opportunity to consolidate their understanding of rigorous concepts so that they can access increasingly complex texts.

Design for Productive Failure

"Failure" may seem antithetical to education, but we consider its presence a quality indicator of task complexity. In much the same way that we recognize that we often learn from our mistakes, so it is with the learners in

According to this standard, students have to discuss the complex texts they have been reading. Not only will this aid them in comprehending the text; it will provide them with practice in critical thinking, argumentation, and using evidence in their responses.

Video 4.5

Students working collaboratively on a presentation.
www.corwin.com/ rigorousreading

our classrooms. The growing research on productive failure in learning is that students who initially fail at a task are more receptive to subsequent instruction, as evidenced by increased achievement and performance (Kapur, 2008). Importantly, we don't want students to experience this failure in isolation. The best time for them to do so is during collaborative learning.

"I'm just not sure they're really doing anything of value when they're in groups." This is perhaps the most frequent reservation we hear from educators when the subject of student collaboration comes up.

A task designed with the possibility of productive failure in mind must be one that is sufficiently novel. In other words, it should not be a mere reproduction of what the teacher just did. A problem with reproductive tasks is that they are susceptible to the "divide and conquer" or the parallel independent work approaches in which so many groups engage. In these scenarios, the task itself is already known; now it's just a matter of students following the steps—no thinking required. Groups with this mindset merely divide up the task, go their separate ways, and then get back together to assemble the final product.

For the task to possess the possibility of productive failure, it must also be designed to require interaction and teamwork. The text students are using should be complex enough that they actually need each other to broker an understanding of it. It is important to listen in on a group that is wrestling with a text that is difficult enough to possibly fail. In doing so, you'll likely hear students discussing the content, not just the task. They will use academic language and vocabulary in ways that indicate they are cognitively engaging with the topic. Ideally, they will also ask questions of one another, offer explanations and clarifications, and provide evidence to support their claims. To be sure, making this quality indicator a reality in your classroom requires getting close to groups to hear how they apply their knowledge to solve problems. But this is essential to more fully understanding the quality of learning that is occurring in your classroom.

Collaborative learning work isn't just pushing four desks together and then calling it a day. A truer measure of the value of collaborative learning hinges on the complexity of a given task and the degree to which students cognitively engage with it. The complexity of the task ensures they have something to talk about; the structure of the task provides them the forum for doing so.

Key Elements of Collaborative Learning

Although there is a strong research base on the effectiveness of peer-assisted learning that takes place in cooperative and collaborative groups, it is also widely recognized that it is challenging to implement the kinds of grouping scenarios that give rise to this learning. Like all good

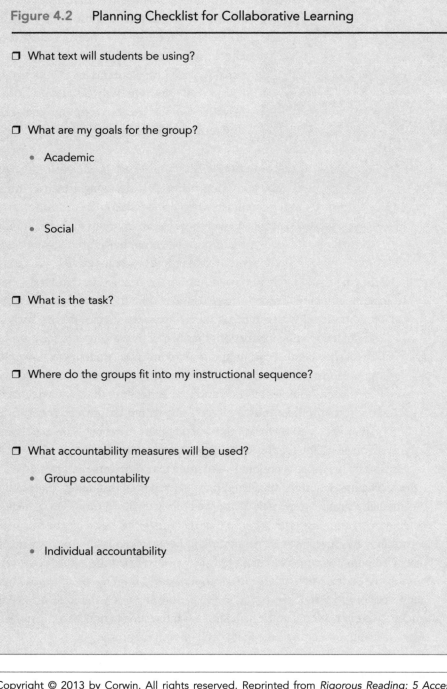

Figure 4.2   Planning Checklist for Collaborative Learning

❑ What text will students be using?

❑ What are my goals for the group?

- Academic

- Social

❑ What is the task?

❑ Where do the groups fit into my instructional sequence?

❑ What accountability measures will be used?

- Group accountability

- Individual accountability

instruction, collaborative learning requires careful planning to ensure success for teachers and students. We have included a checklist in Figure 4.2 for you to use as you consider the key elements of the planning process. Below, we will discuss in more detail those related to grouping, goal setting, and the accountability measures.

Grouping

One of the first decisions a teacher must make when using collaborative learning has to do with how to pair or group students. Should the groups be composed of students working at a similar level (homogeneous grouping) or of differing levels (heterogeneous)? Effective teachers tell us that when they are making grouping decisions, they consider how the group might receive help when faced with a difficult task. In teacher-directed groups such as scaffolded reading instruction, that help is available in the form of the teacher because he or she is working with students at the time. However, in collaborative learning, the students are working apart from the teacher, and help is not as easily obtained. Therefore, the help must emerge from within the group. This help is more likely to occur in mixed-ability pairs or groups. This advantage of mixed-ability groups has been articulated in student feedback as well. In a study of grouping preferences of more than 500 elementary schoolchildren, Elbaum, Schumm, and Vaughn (1997) reported that students preferred mixed-ability groups (especially pairs) to homogeneous groups. On a related note, Bennett and Cass (1989) found that having specific ratios of students with particular ability levels was also important to heterogeneous groups. They noted that the optimal group was composed of two lower-performing students and one higher-performing student. In groups where the ratio was reversed (two higher-performing students to one lower-performing one), the lone struggling student was often left out of the activities. It is interesting to note that the higher-achieving students performed equally well in both circumstances.

Many teachers list the benefits of group work, and then offer an apology: "It just doesn't work for the students I teach."

Goal Setting

Successful collaborative learning pairs or groups understand what their goals are for the task at hand. Be sure to give groups specific directions concerning the task. For example, if they are working together to analyze the structure of an argument put forward by an author, provide them with a rubric describing what you're looking for in the final product that they will be producing. Younger children can benefit from task cards that describe each step in detail. Many students benefit from timelines as well. Multi-step tasks can be broken down into units of time to give a pair or group another way of monitoring their progress.

Accountability

A common criticism of collaborative learning is that the distribution of labor may be uneven. However, this can only occur when there is a flawed accountability system in place. Authorities on this type of instructional arrangement recommend both group and individual accountability measures (Johnson, Johnson, Holubec, & Roy, 1984). This means that student learning should ideally be measured in two ways: first, through a group assessment linked to the completion of the task, and second, through an individual assessment designed to gauge each student's contributions to the effort. Considerations about how you will measure individual accountability should be taken into account when you are building the task itself. Below are some structures for collaborative work that can provide built-in accountability measures.

- **A collaborative poster:** The teacher might assign each member of a group a different colored marker to use in the development of a collaborative poster. In this way, the different colors serve as evidence of each member's contributions.
- **Literature circles:** In literature circles, students' notes typically highlight each member's contributions. It is also common, for instance, to use assigned roles when students are first learning the literature circle format (e.g., the discussion director, vocabulary enricher, etc.) The notes students create during their literature circle meeting can be organized to mirror the roles they are using. As the groups become more proficient, the distinction between the roles can be faded.
- **A discussion roundtable:** Another way to ensure group and individual accountability is through the use of a discussion roundtable. Students can simply fold a

While students may have ample experience with group work in previous grades, they don't yet know how to work for you.

Video 4.6

Students collaborating to learn content.
www.corwin.com/ rigorousreading

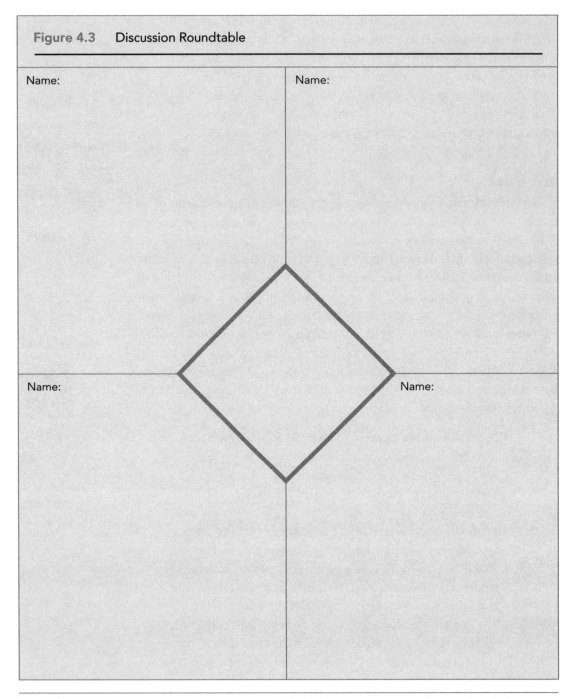

Figure 4.3   Discussion Roundtable

Name:

Name:

Name:

Name:

piece of paper like the one in Figure 4.3. As they read a selected piece of text, they take notes in the upper-left quadrant. They then take turns discussing the text and recording the content that their peers share in the other quadrants. At the end of the conversation they can summarize their understanding of the text, identify the theme, or ask questions (depending on the task assigned the teacher) in the area in the center.

Students who are learning a new way to work with one another should not be challenged with demanding content at the same time.

Student self-assessments are also useful when developing collaborative learning skills in the classroom. Students in secondary school are developmentally more capable of distinguishing between the work of the group and their own role in influencing group dynamics. They can complete an individual feedback sheet that gives them an opportunity to reflect on their contributions and set goals for future collaborative partnerships. These are completed and turned in with the written work. A combination of encouraging students' goal setting and providing them with opportunities for self-evaluation has been shown to improve academic achievement (Schunk, 1998). An example of an individual feedback sheet for older students appears in Figure 4.4. An individual self-assessment for younger students appears in Figure 4.5.

By establishing favorable conditions for collaborative learning, the peer-led portion of class time will run smoothly and result in rewarding exchanges among students. Keep in mind that these collaborative skills should be taught first, through modeling, and that students should then receive feedback about their performance in collaborative tasks. As students become more proficient in the curriculum and self-assessment, they will be prepared to apply them to collaborative learning situations.

When teachers use collaborative learning to help students meet the demands of accessing complex text, the most obvious implication it will have on their instruction will relate to the use of time. Students need time every day, in every class, to practice their collaborative conversations. That's not to say teachers should simply turn over their classrooms to students to talk, but rather that there should be expectations established for student-to-student interaction and that there should be an understanding that students will be held accountable for these interactions.

Figure 4.4 Individual Self-Assessment for Older Students

Name:_____ Date:_____

Name of Project/Assignment: _____

Evaluate your contributions to the collaborative task you completed. Read each statement and circle the number in the column on the right that represents *your* role best.

1 = never

2 = rarely

3 = sometimes

4 = usually

5 = always

I contributed ideas to the discussion.	1	2	3	4	5
I listened to the ideas of others.	1	2	3	4	5
I asked questions.	1	2	3	4	5
I located resources when needed.	1	2	3	4	5
I completed my tasks on time.	1	2	3	4	5
I did my fair share of the work.	1	2	3	4	5

My best contribution to this task was

The next time I work in a group, I will improve on

Based on my assessment, I would give myself a grade of _____.

Figure 4.5 Self-Assessment for Younger Students

Name:_____ Date:_____

Type of Work I Did: _____

Partners' Names: _____

How do I rate my work?

	Always	Sometimes	Not Yet
I asked questions.			
I listened when others talked.			
I did a fair share of the work.			
I used ideas from other people, not just my own.			
I was prepared to work.			

Video 4.7

Teacher
facilitates a
discussion
as practice
for students'
collaborative
work.

*www.corwin.com/
rigorousreading*

▶ Accessing Complex Texts Requires Student-to-Student Interaction

As we have noted, students must learn to interact with one another and the text if they are going to demonstrate proficiency with complex texts. There are a number of different ways to accomplish this, some of which have already been discussed, such as using literature circles and discussion roundtables. The remainder of this chapter provides a review of two additional collaborative learning structures that teachers can use to provide students opportunities to engage with their peers as they access complex texts: reciprocal teaching and collaborative strategic reading.

Reciprocal Teaching

As groups of students read and talk about what they read, they learn more. One structure for facilitating student reading and discussion is reciprocal teaching (Palincsar & Brown, 1984). During reciprocal teaching conversations, students assume practice with a specific comprehension strategy:

- Predicting
- Questioning
- Summarizing
- Clarifying

As they read, they pause periodically and talk about what they are reading. In some cases, they change roles each time they talk. In other cases, they practice the same role throughout the reading. It's important to note that reciprocal teaching groups do not have to consist of four students; students can share a role, or a student can have more than one role. The point of reciprocal teaching is to encourage reading, and deep understanding, of a piece of text. For example, during their discussion of immigration, as part of a unit on industrialization in America, students in Javier Vaca's U.S. history class engaged in reciprocal teaching when they encountered complex texts. Part of the conversation of one group highlights the learning that occurred:

> **Marco:** So, I have a question. What does it mean "push and pull"? What does that have to do with immigration?

Daisy: I think that they're saying that there were things that pushed the immigrants out of their home countries. Like, for example, some people weren't respected because of their religion.

Alexis: Yeah, and then some people were pushed out because they didn't have enough money. That was gonna be part of my summary, because they are saying that when people cannot afford to live in a place, they want to look for a new opportunity.

Uriel: That's the pull, right? Because the U.S. was a place where people could go to get a better life, and make enough money to take care of their family. So, I'll make a prediction. I predict that the next section will tell why that didn't work, because we still have a lot of poverty here, so it couldn't have all worked.

Vanessa: I remember that part where it said that the immigrants thought that "the streets were paved with gold." See, right here [pointing to a place in the text], but they weren't. They were just normal streets, but that was a pull, to think that the U.S. had so much money that they put gold on the street.

The texts used in group work should be more complex than those used in independent reading.

Collaborative Strategic Reading

Collaborative strategic reading (CSR) is a technique used by small groups of heterogeneously grouped students to read and comprehend text (Klinger & Vaughn, 1998). Typically used in groups of five, it is well suited for use with informational text, although it can be used in conjunction with narrative text as well. When using this technique, a text is divided into smaller sections so that the group stops from time to time to discuss what they know so far and what is confusing or unclear. The strength of this approach lies in the use of cooperative learning principles to practice sound comprehension strategies. The following four strategies, which are described in the sections that follow, are used by the group to understand the text:

- Preview
- Click and clunk
- Get the gist
- Wrap up

Collaborative learning should provide students with an opportunity to consolidate their understanding of rigorous concepts so that they can access increasingly complex texts.

Each of these strategies is taught and practiced in a whole-class context until students are able to use them without teacher support. A study of CSR in fourth-grade classrooms found that students who had been carefully taught each of the strategies focused the majority of their talk (65%) on the content of the reading, and another 25% on the procedural aspects of CSR; in contrast, only 2% of their talk was off task (Klinger, Vaughn, & Schumm, 1998).

Before the Reading: Preview

This step is performed before the reading. Students discuss what they already know about the topic of the reading and make predictions about what may be learned in the reading. By creating prediction questions, students can begin to anticipate the information they may encounter during the reading.

During the Reading: Click and Clunk

Click is the term used by the authors to describe smooth reading that makes sense to the student, much like the hum of a well-oiled machine. On the other hand, *clunk* describes the times when a reader encounters an unfamiliar word or concept. Together, clicks and clunks represent self-monitoring behaviors used by fluent readers. The clunks signal to the readers that other strategies for resolving comprehension problems are needed. After noticing that a problem has occurred, the reader can

- *reread* the sentence or paragraph;
- *read ahead* until the end of the sentence or paragraph;
- *analyze* the word for familiar affixes or root words; or
- *ask* his or her partner what it means.

During CSR, students read a passage from the text then discuss their clunks. Using their collective knowledge, they clarify each other's understanding of the word or concept in question.

During the Reading: Get the Gist

At the end of each section of the passage, students summarize the main ideas and important facts. Like prediction and self-monitoring, summarizing is a comprehension behavior used by fluent readers (Brown & Day, 1983). Both click and clunk and get the gist are repeated several times until the entire reading has been completed.

After the Reading: Wrap Up

Once the group has finished with the reading, they revisit the predictions they made to check for accuracy. They also generate questions and answers that focus on the main ideas and important facts.

Students are initially assigned roles in CSR so that the discussion will flow more smoothly, and in time, these distinctions are faded as groups become more proficient with the process. These roles include the following:

Students who initially fail at a task are more receptive to subsequent instruction.

- **Leader:** makes sure the strategies are used and seeks help from the teacher when needed
- **Clunk expert:** leads discussion on how to figure out unknown words or concepts
- **Announcer:** makes sure everyone has a chance to participate
- **Reporter:** shares the group's work during the "share" portion of the language arts workshop
- **Timer:** monitors the time so the group can complete the task during collaborative learning

A group of third-grade students used CSR with the picture book *Stick Out Your Tongue!* (Bonsignore, 2001). An excerpt of the book read,

> Moths and butterflies use their tongues like straws to suck the sweet nectar from flowers.
>
> The tongue of an insect like a moth or butterfly is quite different from the tongues of other animals. These insects have a proboscis, a mouthpart that extends out and forms a long, thin tube much like a tiny straw. The moth or butterfly sticks the proboscis deep into the heart of the flower blossom and sucks the sweet nectar. One moth in Madagascar has a proboscis that is nine inches long! That's about as long as your mom's foot! (p. 3)

Ting, the leader of the group, asked everyone to read the page, then called on Kimberly, the clunk expert, to start the discussion about difficult vocabulary. "Did anyone have a clunk—a tricky word?"

"I had a bunch of them," said Marvin. Alicia, the announcer, reminded him to pick one so that everyone would have a turn. "I pick this word, then," said Marvin, pointing to *proboscis*. "I don't even know how to say it!"

Kimberly followed. "I had trouble with that one, too. Let's look at the list to see how we can figure it out. Let's reread the sentence." After all of them finished rereading, Marvin exclaimed, "There it is! It's 'a mouthpart that extends out and forms a long, thin tube.' It's right here in the picture." He points to the illustration of a moth using his proboscis to suck nectar from the center of a daisy.

"The illustrator even drew a picture of a boy drinking from a straw to remind us of how it works," offered Wilfredo. The leader continued the conversation, and the group discussed *blossom* (Marvin knew this word), *nectar* (they made a connection to *nectarine* and decided it was something sweet), and *Madagascar* (they used context clues to determine that it was a place, then consulted an atlas to pinpoint its location).

Wilfredo, the timer, reminded the group that they needed to "get the gist" if they were going to finish this passage. After discussing the main idea of the passage, they each wrote the following sentence in their journal:

> Moths and butterflies use a proboscis to suck nectar from flowers.

After reading three more pages of the book together, the group had developed several summary sentences, which they incorporated into their written summary of the book.

▶ Summary

Gaining access to complex text requires collaborative conversations because students need to talk about texts and make meaning with their peers. In previous chapters, we explained how modeling academic discourse is a vital first step in fostering critical thinking. Students then begin to apply this discourse under the watchful eye of the teacher during close reading and scaffolded reading. But without opportunities to use this on their own during collaborative learning, students don't get the chance to practice how they "talk" to themselves as they read complex text independently. Collaborative learning, whether through literature circles, discussion roundtables, reciprocal teaching, or collaborative strategic reading, gives students the time they need to witness their own thinking and learn about the ideas of others.

The text students are using should be complex enough that they actually need each other to broker an understanding of it.

Access Point Four

An Independent Reading Staircase

Although it is independent reading time in Mrs. Garcia's fourth-grade class, it is far from silent. Several children are clustered in a comfortable corner of the room where rocking chairs and braided rugs offer an inviting space to get lost in a book. Others students are reading at their tables on iPads. Trisha and Leon are looking through a basket in the classroom library labeled *Gold Rush Books*, while Kaleem, Sonje, and Melissa are already reading. The pages of their books sprout sticky notes with handwritten annotations.

While most of the students are settling into their independent reading, Mrs. Garcia is seated at a small table in another corner of the room. To her left are a binder for her student reading conference notes and a stack of observation forms like the one in Figure 5.1. Patrice, a girl with braids and a quick smile, is discussing her book with her teacher.

"Tell me about the book you're reading, Patrice. What has happened so far?" asks Mrs. Garcia.

Figure 5.1   Reading Conference Form

Student Reading Conference

Name: _____   Date: _____

Title and Author: _____

Retelling (check all that apply)

- ❑ discusses important events
- ❑ offers salient details
- ❑ uses evidence from the text to support retelling
- ❑ states opinion
- ❑ provides textual support for opinion
- ❑ needs prompts to expand answers

Notes:

Oral Reading Fluency

- ❑ reads accurately
- ❑ fluently, in long phrases
- ❑ choppy, in short phrases
- ❑ word by word
- ❑ with expression
- ❑ flat and without expression

Notes:

Goals for Next Meeting

"It's really good!" offers Patrice.

> I'm reading *Seeds of Hope* [Gregory, 2001], and it's about a girl named Susanna who is traveling on a ship to get to Oregon. Her mom died on the ship, and her dad lost all their money. Now they're going to go to California because they heard about gold.

This novel, told in diary form, has been a popular choice among many of the students in the class during the last few weeks.

After asking a few more questions to confirm Patrice's comprehension, Mrs. Garcia asks her to read a passage that was meaningful to her. Patrice chooses the journal entry when Susanna's father tells her they will be going to California instead of Oregon. While Patrice reads, Mrs. Garcia makes notes about Patrice's reading fluency and her use of expression. Mrs. Garcia then asks Patrice about observations she has made during the reading. Patrice turns to the section of the book about when Susanna's father tells her he is going to be a gold miner, not a doctor.

> I was thinking about another book I read this year called *Riding Freedom* [Ryan, 1999]. Susanna reminds me of Charley in *Riding Freedom* because she has to learn how to rely on herself when her parents aren't there for her anymore.

A guiding principle of the Common Core is that students should achieve a level of independence that makes it possible for them to express their own thoughts and ideas and to understand the thoughts and ideas of others.

As their reading conference draws to an end, Mrs. Garcia and Patrice develop a goal for Patrice to look for historical connections since they are studying the California Gold Rush in social studies. With that, Patrice leaves the table with her book in hand. Looking back over her shoulder, Patrice remarks, "I'll let you know what happens next!"

A guiding principle of the Common Core State Standards is that students should achieve a level of independence that makes it possible for them to express their own thoughts and ideas and to understand the thoughts and ideas of others. Marie Clay (2001) refers to this as "the high demand from the first days of school for children to read and write texts according to their competencies but always as independently as possible" (p. 48). After all, as educators, our intent is to develop a set of skills in each learner that ultimately can be used outside the presence of the teacher. Like all aspects of learning, each student's ability to engage in independent tasks is fostered through explicit instruction.

An important advantage of developing independent learners is that the teacher can then use his or her time to support the efforts of individual students. Within every class, there exist some students who need more specialized teacher supports; as well, every student, regardless of achievement level, needs personal contact with the teacher. As busy classroom teachers know, this can happen on a consistent basis only when all the students know how to work collaboratively and independently. A powerful practice for making contact with each student is known as *conferring*. Teachers confer with students through rich conversations about their reading practices.

This chapter focuses on the roles of students and teachers as they access complex texts during independent learning. While students work independently to apply the literacy skills and strategies they have been taught during modeling, close reading, scaffolded reading instruction, and collaborative learning, teachers are conferring with students individually to engage them in important conversations about their learning.

An important advantage of developing independent learners is that the teacher can then use his or her time to support the efforts of individual students.

The Goals of Independent Learning

It seems as if the practice of having students working quietly and independently on individual tasks is as old a concept as school itself. Many of us have memories of toiling away on worksheets while the teacher walked up and down the aisles. Rarely were any words exchanged, other than those pertaining to simple questions about the assignment at hand. When completed, these worksheets were turned in to be graded. Rarely did we understand how any of these worksheets connected to our learning. The goal instead seemed to be to complete the workbook or the pile of dittos in our folders.

There are several drawbacks associated with this approach to independent work. For one, the work completed independently may focus on many repetitions of the same isolated skills, leading to disengagement and boredom. This is especially true for struggling readers who will sometimes focus on getting the assignment done rather than on the intended learning outcomes that were built into the lesson design (Anderson, Brubaker, Alleman-Brooks, & Duffy, 1985). For example, envision the student who

Video 5.1

Doug discusses independent learning.
www.corwin.com/ rigorousreading

completes a spelling assignment of writing each word 10 times by instead writing each letter in a vertical column of 10 until the entire word is completed. After completing the list, the student is no closer to remembering how to spell the word than when she began. When we talk about independent learning, we are not referring to activities like worksheets intended to keep students quiet and occupied. The goal of independent learning is to empower students to develop self-regulation skills, increase their sense of competence, and set goals for themselves. Below, we discuss these three goals in greater detail.

Self-Regulation

Independent learning provides students with opportunities to self-regulate—to manage their time, monitor their progress, and solve problems. In their study of third graders, Stright and Supplee (2002) found that students were more likely to ask for help and monitor their progress during independent learning when they had been taught how to do so. Good and Brophy (2003) consider self-regulation to be an essential component of the curriculum:

A powerful practice for making contact with each student is known as conferring. Teachers confer with students through rich conversations about their reading practices.

> Students cannot learn self-regulation and self-control if the teacher does all of the alerting, accountability, and so on. They need to be taught to manage time (we have fifteen minutes to finish a task) and to define their own work and procedures (what is the critical problem—how else might the problem be approached?) This appropriate management necessitates that rules and structures—the scaffolding–be progressively altered to encourage more responsibility for self-control. (p. 137)

When students have daily opportunities to engage in meaningful independent learning, they not only apply literacy skills and strategies but also develop the ability to regulate and monitor their pace of work and hone their problem-solving skills.

Competence

In addition to helping students self-regulate, independent learning provides them with a chance to develop a sense of competence. The concept of competence hinges on a learner's perception of her abilities and on her understanding of the effort needed to accomplish a task. While many speak of the importance of self-esteem in the learning process, it is *competenc*e that really contributes to a learner's self-esteem. It is through a sense of competence that self-esteem is built. This, in turn, increases motivation, because we are motivated to do those things we know we do well. When students have the opportunity to explore and experience their own competence through independent learning, their self-efficacy improves, and they begin to believe that learning is under their control (Yeager & Dweck, 2012).

When we talk about independent learning, we are not referring to activities like worksheets intended to keep students quiet and occupied.

Goal Setting

A final positive aspect of independent learning is that it allows students to gain experience at setting and achieving goals. Alexander and Jetton (2000, p. 297) describe students as possessing one or more of the following goal orientations that serve to propel or inhibit their learning.

- **Performance goals:** Students who view learning through this lens are interested in teacher recognition and good grades. The extrinsic rewards of the task become the goal for completing the work.
- **Mastery goals:** Students with this orientation are interested in the content of the task and the opportunity to expand their own knowledge base.
- **Work-avoidant goals:** Some students are primarily interested in completing the task with the least amount of effort necessary.

All students are motivated by a combination of these goals to varying degrees. However, it is important to recognize that all of these orientations exist and that the second category—that of the mastery goals—is the one that teachers should aim to cultivate. Independent learning provides teachers with the perfect opportunity to make this happen, as this is a format in which students will experience many opportunities to set their own goals and monitor their progress toward attaining them. In addition, the practice of independent learning provides teachers with opportuninities to monitor their students—through conferring—throughout the learning process.

▶ Accessing Complex Texts Requires Independent Reading

One way to ensure that students read in class is to provide them with time to read. Unlike silent sustained reading in which students read texts of their own choosing, independent reading constrains students' choices, and they read increasingly complex texts. For example, earth science teacher Adam Renick provides 10 minutes each day for his students to independently read complex texts about the content they are studying. Mr. Renick notes, "Scientists read every day as part of their job, and I want my students to have that same experience." Reading widely builds background knowledge and vocabulary, which is essential for strengthening disciplinary knowledge. Students can't draw on personal experiences alone when learning about the physical, social, and biological world, particularly as the content grows more technical in middle school. They must read complex texts that develop their knowledge. There is evidence that when students are provided with time for independent reading of content-area-aligned texts, their academic performance improves (Fisher, Ross, & Grant, 2010).

Students were more likely to ask for help and monitor their progress during independent learning when they had been taught how to do so.

To understand complex texts, students must master content-area knowledge. They should view reading as a means of gaining such knowledge. Stated a different way, knowledge cannot be built simply by telling students what they need to know. They need to see texts as an important source of information. Thoughtfully chosen independent reading materials afford students with opportunities to (1) apply what they have been taught about comprehension, and (2) build their knowledge about the topics they are studying. As noted in the Common Core State Standards, "Standard 10 defines a grade-by-grade 'staircase' of increasing text complexity that rises from beginning reading to the college and career readiness level" (CCSS, 2010, p. 80).

This staircase has to be built over years, as well as over units of study and phases of instruction. The texts selected for independent reading on a given day should be complex, but perhaps not as complex as those used during close reading or scaffolded reading that occurs on the same day. However, there should be a steady, forward progression in the complexity of texts used in independent reading and collaborative conversations; this progression should mirror the trajectory of increasing text complexity followed when engaging in close readings.

Independent reading is important because students need time to try on the strategies they have been learning. Thus, the practice of independent reading is connected with the modeling and scaffolded instruction students have received. The effectiveness of independent reading is rooted in two concepts: increasing reading volume and developing positive reading attitudes.

Reading Volume

Reading volume is a measure of the amount of reading a learner engages in both in school and at home. Stanovich (1986) examined the relationship between students' volume of outside reading and their ability to read. This study confirmed what many teachers had always known—the more reading students do, the better their reading becomes. A related study compared students' standardized test scores in reading and the amount of outside reading they did. As in the earlier study, the results indicated that there was a strong correlation between reading volume and achievement (Anderson, Wilson, & Fielding, 1988). A table of the results can be seen in Figure 5.2. These and similar studies spurred educators' interest in carving out a portion of the school day during which students could read independently for an extended period of time.

Positive Reading Attitudes

In addition to exploring the connection between reading and achievement, studies have demonstrated the importance of positive reading attitudes. Concern over this topic is well founded because positive student attitudes toward reading decline during the late elementary years, especially among boys (Kush & Watkins, 1996). A large-scale study based on national testing results suggested that students who had positive attitudes toward reading (described as *engaged readers*) outperformed older, disengaged readers (Campbell, Voekl, & Donahue, 1997). An analysis of fourth graders' results on the same test revealed that engaged readers from low-income backgrounds outperformed disengaged readers from higher socioeconomic backgrounds (Guthrie, Schafer, & Huang, 2001). These positive attitudes toward reading are developed through

When students have the opportunity to explore and experience their own competence through independent learning, their self-efficacy improves, and they begin to believe that learning is under their control.

Figure 5.2 Relationship Between Achievement and Independent Reading

Percentile Rank	Minutes of Reading per Day (Books)	Words Read per Year
98	65.0	4,358,000
90	21.1	1,823,000
80	14.2	1,146,000
70	9.6	622,000
60	6.5	432,000
50	4.6	282,000
40	3.2	200,000
30	1.8	106,000
20	0.7	21,000
10	0.1	8,000
2	0.0	0

Source: Adapted from Anderson et al. (1988). Used with permission.

- clear learning goals;
- texts that relate to a student's personal experiences;
- support from the teacher on making choices;
- texts with interesting topics;
- instruction in reading strategies;
- opportunities to collaborate with other students;

- a positive environment that is not driven by extrinsic rewards;
- evaluation that provides feedback on progress, rather than tests of knowledge;
- personal connections to the teacher; and
- cohesive instruction. (Guthrie & Wigfield, 2000)

Differences Between SSR and Independent Reading

There are some differences between sustained silent reading (SSR) and independent reading, although both of them have their place in the classroom. In particular, they differ in terms of overall purpose, book selection and access, accountability, and roles of the student and teacher. A summary of these differences can be seen in Figure 5.3.

Goals and Purpose. The primary goal of SSR is to develop positive student attitudes toward reading and to encourage students to view reading as a recreational activity. On the other hand, the goal of independent reading is to provide time for practice of skills and strategies taught in other phases of instruction.

Book Selection. In SSR, the student makes the ultimate decision about what he or she will read. The teacher provides guidance and information about choosing books that are a "good fit," but a student is never discouraged from reading a particular book. In independent reading, the teacher has more influence over what will be read because the text should connect to the content being taught. In addition, the independent reading text should build the reading prowess of students, taking them up another step on their staircase to accessing complex texts.

Book Access. During independent reading, a narrow range of texts are made available because the purpose is to practice using a skill or strategy. In SSR, students have access to and read a wide range of materials, including nontraditional texts like comic books, magazines, and web-based information.

Accountability. During independent reading, students spend some of their time completing reading logs, graphic organizers, précis writing, and written reflections about the reading. In SSR, nonaccountability is the hallmark. Students simply read.

Figure 5.3 Differences Between SSR and Independent Reading

	Sustained Silent Reading	Independent Reading
Goals and purpose	• Reading for pleasure	• Building mastery through practice
Book selection	• Student choice with a wide range of genres and levels	• Constrained choice of increasingly complex texts
Accountability	• No records kept	• Logs and reflections are essential
What are students doing?	• Reading quietly	• Reading and writing reflections • Conferring with teacher
What is the teacher doing?	• Brief book talk • Reading quietly	• Conferring with students • Observing • Assessing
Follow-up activity	• Students can volunteer to briefly talk about a book; this is not always a part of an SSR session	• Students discuss their reading. The discussion is related to the purpose set at the beginning of the session

Student's Role. During SSR, students read until the end of the time allotted, then transition to the next activity. During independent reading, students may be reading, writing about their reading, or conferring with the teacher about their reading.

Teacher's Role. During SSR, the teacher reads to provide an adult model of recreational reading. During independent reading, the teacher is conferring with students, assessing and observing while students read.

Follow-Up Activities. In SSR, students may be invited to share a book they are reading. However, this is never a requirement, and students are

free to volunteer or not. In independent reading, a sharing phase is included at the end of each reading period. The discussions students engage in during this sharing phase are based on the assignment that was given to them before the independent reading began.

Students Respond During Independent Reading

One of the goals of independent reading is to provide students with an opportunity to write about thoughts, ideas, and evidence that connect to their reading. These written responses are usually brief in nature, and teachers can use a variety of tools with their students to help them organize their thoughts as they are writing. We have included several samples of these tools at the end of this chapter to provide you with examples of reading logs and comment cards for a range of grade levels.

Unlike silent sustained reading in which students read texts of their own choosing, independent reading constrains students' choices, and they read increasingly complex texts.

Reading Logs

Nearly all teachers want students to keep track of the books they have read during independent reading, and nearly all students need a way to organize that information. Reading logs are best kept simple so that students spend the majority of time reading rather than on clerical tasks. A simple reading log appears in Figure 5.4. Students can easily reproduce this in a spiral notebook kept for independent reading.

Emergent and early readers need a simpler format for keeping track of their reading. The example in Figure 5.5 is more appropriate for students who are still mastering writing. This reading log can be stored on a clipboard for ease of writing.

Comment Cards

Students use these simple note taking frameworks to jot down thoughts and ideas related to the strategies and skills they are practicing or the content they are learning. This is an early form of annotation for students who are just beginning to learn this skill. A sample comment card appears in Figure 5.6.

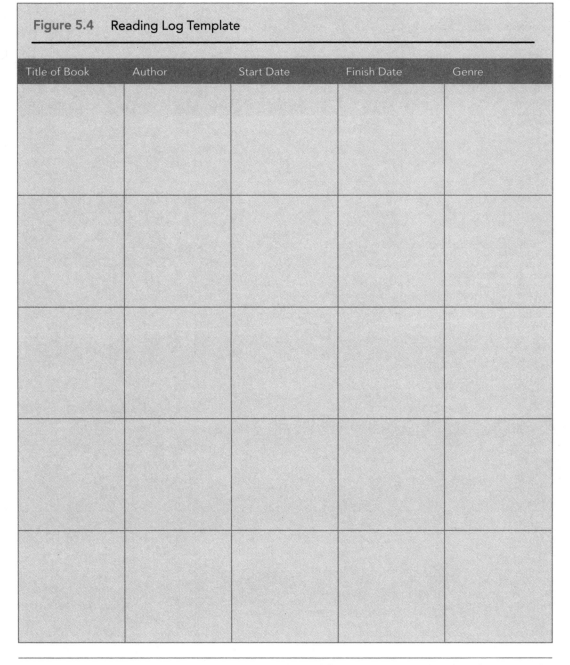

Figure 5.4   Reading Log Template

Title of Book	Author	Start Date	Finish Date	Genre

Figure 5.5   Reading Log for Younger Readers

Name: _____

Title of Book	Author	Did you like it?
		☺ 😐 ☹
		☺ 😐 ☹
		☺ 😐 ☹
		☺ 😐 ☹
		☺ 😐 ☹
		☺ 😐 ☹
		☺ 😐 ☹
		☺ 😐 ☹

For example, Aida Allen asked her fifth graders to look for evidence of foreshadowing during independent reading. Jeremy reviewed the previous chapters he had already read and wrote several notes on his comment card about *Frindle* (Clements, 1996; see Figure 5.7).

Sticky Notes

As students become more adept at making notes as they are reading—and if they are not allowed to annotate directly on the text—they can move from comment cards to sticky notes. These small notes can be positioned to "underline" important passages students encounter. A challenge of using sticky notes is teaching students how to use them with an economy of words. Learners who have been accustomed to writing on 8-1/2" × 11" sheets of paper may attempt to crowd too many words onto these small notes. It is useful for them to have a bank of simple annotations available to help them abbreviate their thoughts while still preserving meaning.

Reflection Journals

Independent readers not only read for meaning; they also need to reflect on and discuss their readings with others. To support their discussions, students need to make notes and write down their thoughts and observations. The purpose for reading should be established at the beginning of the independent reading time, with appropriate instruction about what to look for in the reading. Many teachers find that instructing students to begin notes from each reading session on a new page of a reflection journal (complete with date, title, and relevant page numbers) is helpful for keeping students organized. These response journal entries can address a range of topics, but generally offer students the opportunities to engage in a meaningful transaction with the text. Students can then draw from the content of these reflection journals during class discussions to provide evidence from the texts they are reading; these journals are also read by the teacher.

Readers make meaning at the word level through understanding the vocabulary, and at the sentence and paragraph levels through understanding how ideas are crafted by the author to tell a story or forward a position on a topic. But readers also make meaning through their own transactions with the text. They activate their background knowledge to determine the veracity of the text—"Could this happen?" Finally, they analyze the text for

Video 5.3

Teachers talk about the use of independent reading.
www.corwin.com/ rigorousreading

When students are provided with time for independent reading of content-area-aligned texts, their academic performance improves.

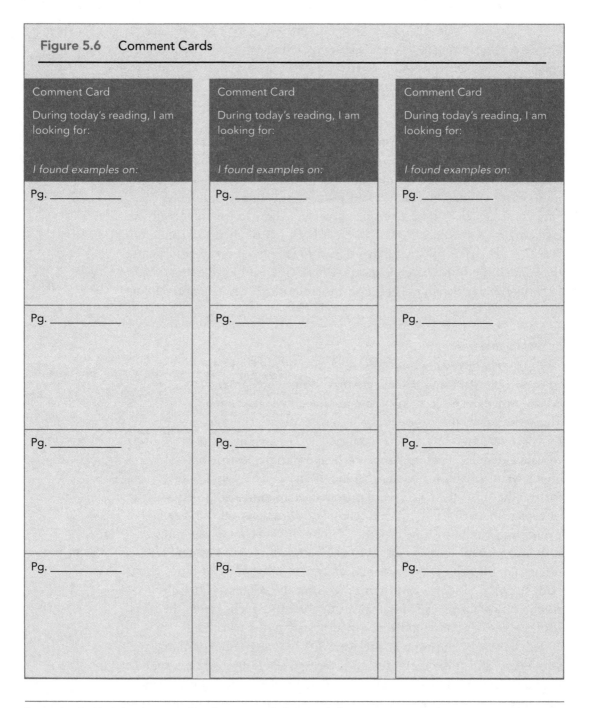

Figure 5.6   Comment Cards

Comment Card	Comment Card	Comment Card
During today's reading, I am looking for:	During today's reading, I am looking for:	During today's reading, I am looking for:
I found examples on:	*I found examples on:*	*I found examples on:*
Pg. _____	Pg. _____	Pg. _____
Pg. _____	Pg. _____	Pg. _____
Pg. _____	Pg. _____	Pg. _____
Pg. _____	Pg. _____	Pg. _____

Figure 5.7   Jeremy's Comment Card

Comment Card

During today's reading, I am looking for:

foreshadowing

I found examples on:

Pg. **1**

Was Nick a troublemaker? Hard to say.

Pg. **8**

Mrs. Granger didn't just enjoy the dictionary. She <u>loved</u> the dictionary—almost worshipped it.

Pg. **12**

It was still a week before school and Nick already felt like fifth grade was going to be a very long year.

Pg. _____

its usefulness to them—"What did I learn from this text?" In other words, the words on the page do not simply lie there waiting to be consumed without analysis by the reader. Instead, there is a transaction that occurs between the text and the reader that makes each text–reader relationship unique. This is why, for example, one person can love a book while another considers it a complete waste of time.

Those transactions form the basis for reader response theory (Rosenblatt, 1938/1995). Reader response theory suggests that all reading experiences can be described as a balance between efferent (information-seeking) and aesthetic (emotional) responses. It is important to note that one is not more valued than another, but rather that each reading experience can be represented on a continuum between these two response types. For example, a reader's response to Robert Frost's poem "Stopping By Woods on a Snowy Evening" may be primarily aesthetic as the reader enjoys how Frost crafts his words and meter. However, there is still likely to be an efferent component as the reader constructs his understanding of the woods. At the other extreme, a reader's response to the book *How Animals Shed Their Skin* (Tatham, 2002) may be primarily efferent as he or she look for information about leopard frogs. Even then, there is likely to be an aesthetic response as well when they view the weird and wonderful animals in the photographs. Although it is not necessary to teach students these terms (we shudder at the thought of a second grader offering, "I would like to make an aesthetic response to *Madeline*"), it is important that they have many opportunities to explore their transactions with the texts they are reading. As they gain insight into the way they are interacting with the texts, they will become conscious of their learning and build their metacognitive skills. In addition, this awareness will also feed into their ability to understand their levels of comprehension and self-monitor accordingly.

Knowledge cannot be built simply by telling students what they need to know. They need to see texts as an important source of information.

Students Talk About Texts

One of the desired outcomes of independent reading is that students will talk about the texts they are reading in collaborative conversations. These conversations can take place in small-group collaborative sessions or in a whole-class format. Providing students with time to share offers numerous benefits for readers. First, it is useful for oral language development at both the social and content levels. For English language learners in particular, it is an occasion to engage in academic language. Book discussions also provide opportunities for students to hone listening skills, particularly when they are encouraged to make connections to peers' comments rather than to direct their conversations to the teacher. These collaborative conversations are critical for helping students clarify their understanding of a text, ask questions, and deepen their understanding of complex texts. As with all aspects of instruction, it should never be assumed that students know how to participate in rich discussions about a text. Therefore, these skills should be explicitly taught so that students can begin to fully participate in this academic discourse.

An example of a collaborative conversation follows:

It is early October, and the students in Lisa Targas's first-grade classroom have been reading sequence stories to understand how an author can tell a tale that builds on the action. During her modeling, Ms. Targas used *Joseph Had a Little Overcoat* (Tayback, 1999) to chart the sequence of events that occurred as Joseph's coat became more worn and was converted into a jacket, vest, tie, patch, and button. During collaborative reading, students worked in small groups to create similar charts for *There Was an Old Lady Who Swallowed a Fly* (Tayback, 2007).

The texts selected for independent reading on a given day should be complex, but perhaps not as complex as those used during close reading or scaffolded reading that occurs on the same day.

After multiple experiences with sequence texts, students were ready to read and discuss others during independent reading. Ms. Targas created a box full of books with stories that use sequence as a major feature. Students selected titles and created their own sequence charts, using a format similar to the one seen in Figure 5.8. While all of the students worked, Ms. Targas met with select individual students to confer about their work and also offered support for others who needed clarification on their reading.

When students finished reading and responding, they began to discuss the books they had chosen. Ms. Targas prompted,

> Remember to use your journals because that's where you have some of your good ideas written down. We're going to start by talking about the books you read. We paid attention to the sequences in our stories today so let's start there. Who would like to begin?

Figure 5.8   Reading Journal Format for Sequence Stories

Title of book: _____   Author: _____

This book was about

The best part of this book was

One way the author could change this book is

Here's what happened in the text (use pictures and words)

1	2	3
4	5	6

The class discussed the plots of the stories and the sequences used. Stephanie remarked that her book, *The Napping House* (Wood, 2009), reminded her of the time the ceiling fan fell down in the living room one night and woke everyone in the house. As the students discussed the content, Ms. Targas made notes about students' performance. These notes serve as fodder for future instruction, including the individual conferences that she will have with her students.

Video 5.4

Nancy discusses the role of conferencing during reading.
www.corwin.com/ rigorousreading

▶ Accessing Complex Texts Requires Conferring

When students are reading or writing independently, the teacher can use some of this time to meet individually with students. Conferring provides the teacher with an excellent assessment opportunity. These conferences allow the teacher to gauge the progress of each student, clarify information, and provide feedback for next steps. In addition, teachers keep records of these conversations for later reflection about individual student progress. These conferences are brief in nature (a few minutes or so) and can be used as a follow up to inform further scaffolded instruction. Teachers usually average between three and five student conferences per independent reading session.

Effective conferences include four elements. Because each conference event is short, these elements come into play very quickly. When conferring, the student and teacher use the learner's work as evidence. The teacher focuses on only one or two points during a single session. A helpful sequence for a conference is as follows:

The effectiveness of independent reading is rooted in two concepts: increasing reading volume and developing positive reading attitudes.

- **Inquiry:** The teacher begins by conversing with the student about his or her work. The goal is to assess the student on one literacy focus topic per session.
- **Decisions:** Based on the evidence culled from the opening conversation, the teacher rapidly makes a decision about what should be taught next.
- **Instruction:** The teacher provides a minute or two of procedural, literary, or strategic instruction to help the student move to the next level of independent learning, and the student attempts the work with teacher support.

- **Recordkeeping:**
  The teacher makes anecdotal notes about the main points of the conference.

The notes generated from these conferences will be consulted again later for further instructional and evaluative decisions. It is not uncommon for teachers to customize their conferring forms to meet the unique needs of their classrooms. However, a basic format for a conference appears in Figure 5.9.

The goal of a reading conference is to engage a student in a conversation about the book he or she is reading. The purpose of the conference is determined by the teacher and student together because the conversation should be a give-and-take of questions and ideas. In any case, the student and teacher should use both the text and reading journal during the conversation. The scenario at the beginning of this chapter is a reading conference. Useful goals for a reading conference include the following:

- Discuss something in the text.
- Ask about areas of confusion.
- Discuss the author's purpose or craft.
- Review the student's list of books read.
- Set reading goals together.

▶ Summary

Independent reading is a time when students get to practice applying what they have been learning during other parts of the instructional day or unit of study. Typically, students read a book that has been selected by the teacher because it features opportunities for them to use or draw from techniques or content they have already been learning. Students may respond in a reading journal and then use these notes to participate in discussions with other students. Teachers and students confer about independent reading and writing. The goal of these conferences

Figure 5.9   Overview Form for Conferences

Name	Date	Type of Conference	Topic Discussed	Next Meeting	Goal for Next Meeting

Types of conferences:
  RC: reading conference
  WC: writing conference
  O: other (specify)

Researchers have confirmed what many teachers already know— the more reading students do, the better their reading becomes.

is to engage students in an individual conversation about their work. A useful sequence for teachers to use during a conference is to first inquire, then make decisions about the immediate needs of the student. Teachers should be sure to note important details of the conference for next time and to end the session with a goal that the student can accomplish. When students read independently and confer with their teachers about the texts they are reading, they begin to access complex texts in new ways, ways that build the habits necessary for them to read for meaning in college and throughout their careers.

Access Point Five

Demonstrating Understanding and Assessing Performance

Students love to make personal connections with the texts they are reading. If you've ever heard a student say, "This is just like the time I ..." you've experienced this firsthand. Personal connections are important for reading engagement. As Buehl (2009) noted, "[S]tudents can see how their personal lives intersect with what an author tells them" (p. 42). But personal connections alone are not sufficient if students are to fully understand a given text. Students also need to understand what the author is saying, both literally and figuratively. Unfortunately, too many students have not been taught how to return to their reading and analyze the text. They have been allowed—encouraged, even—to focus on what the text means to them, to the exclusion of fully understanding what the author is stating and how it is situated within a particular historical, scientific, or social context. Consider the following exchange that took place with a student who was new to our school. Drew's class was learning about genetics and heredity.

Drew:	I didn't know you could get a heart attack from your family.
Ms. Alexander:	Tell me more about that. What are you thinking?
Drew:	My grandpa had a heart attack. I remember when we went to see him at the hospital. He had all of these tubes, and they cut his chest open. He got a big scar right here [pointing to this chest and drawing a line down to his abdomen].
Ms. Alexander:	Are you reading about heart disease being inherited?
Drew:	Yeah. And then the doctor said that he had to go on a special diet and not eat too much fat foods. Like now he eats fish, vegetables, rice, apples, yogurt, and stuff like that. So I guess my dad will have a heart problem, and then I will later on, like maybe when I'm 50 or so.
Ms. Alexander:	But what does the author say about that? Reread the section on environmental influences for me.
Drew:	[returning to the text for the first time] It says that heart problems can be inherited.
Ms. Alexander:	And what else? Please read on.
Drew:	It says that diet and exercise also are important.
Ms. Alexander:	So the author says that diet and exercise contribute to the occurrence and seriousness of the disease.

Unfortunately, too many students have been allowed— encouraged, even— to focus on what the text means to them, to the exclusion of fully understanding what the author is stating.

Drew:	Yeah, they make my grandpa exercise, too.
Ms. Alexander:	I think that the author is saying that some people may not have heart attacks if they eat right and exercise. It's not just about what happens after the heart attack. It's also what you do that can lead up to heart disease.
Drew:	Really? Are you sure?

As is very common in classrooms, students like Drew fail to notice the author's message and instead choose a little part of the text to focus on and then make personal. In this case, unchecked, Drew would have been convinced that heart attacks are entirely hereditary, that he will end up having a heart attack, and that there isn't anything people can do to prevent heart disease. While not all personal connections forged with a text involve completely ignoring an author's message or misinterpreting it to this same degree, many result in significant misconceptions and errors in understanding.

▶ Accessing Complex Texts Requires More Than Personal Connections

What, then, should happen in a classroom to prevent students from relying only on personal connections while they are reading? How can teachers refocus students on the text and ensure that they understand the author's message? If you recall from previous chapters, there are specific teacher behaviors that allow students to access complex texts. As a reminder, the Common Core State Standards require that students learn to use textual evidence, compare texts, and analyze how an author unfolds a series of ideas or theses. Below, we will discuss four ways teachers can help students refocus on the text:

- Model before you expect.
- Pose questions that require students to return to the text.
- Ask students to provide evidence to support their opinions and ideas.
- Require students to write rhetorically.

Model before you expect. As with everything we want students to learn, teachers must model the process of returning to a text to determine the author's purpose and perspective. Readers don't always have to agree with the information presented by the author, but they must understand the information presented by the author before they can counter it. As we noted in Chapter 2, students deserve to hear examples of their teachers completing the cognitive tasks they are asked to do. For example, while reading a social studies text, the teacher might say, "The author says that there are several reasons for economic decline. I have my own ideas, but I have to think about what the author is saying first so that I can decide if I agree or not."

Teachers must model the process of returning to a text to determine the author's purpose and perspective.

Pose questions that require students to return to the text. Students are unlikely to return to the text if they are not asked to do so. A line of questioning that encourages students to read closely for details they may have overlooked during the first reading ensures students return to the text regularly. Some of these questions may be detail oriented, but the majority should invite students to use the resources at hand. For example, the biology teacher says,

> Take a look at the diagram of the stages of meiosis on page 149. What happens between the anaphase II stage and telophase II? There are some important changes that are happening there. Let's look closely at it and see if we can figure it out.

As students strive to answer questions that require them to examine and analyze a text, they will develop the habit of persistence that they need to understand difficult concepts that they might otherwise dismiss as being too hard.

Ask students to provide evidence to support their opinions and ideas. To be sure, asking students to make connections between a text and their personal experiences can be a way of initially establishing some relevance. A real strength of learners is their quest for broader truths in life, and the content they learn in school should inform their personal perspectives and help them along this journey. However, dwelling on personal connections can also stall students' learning if they are not required to then move beyond their experiences to gain a broader understanding of the world. When unfettered in this way, students may be given to absolutes that may not be moored to

Video 6.1

Teacher reflects on her close reading instruction.
www.corwin.com/ rigorousreading

anything substantial. Therefore, when a student offers an opinion or idea, the teacher or a peer should probe further by asking for evidence to substantiate the claim. This shouldn't be a hostile move, but rather one that encourages students to return to the reading material. When a teacher says to a student, "Show me where you found that," he's asking the student to return to the text to provide evidence. When the teacher follows by saying, "Read that to all of us so we can talk about it together," the teacher is establishing the discourse necessary for meaningful, text-based discussion.

Students are unlikely to return to the text if they are not asked to do so.

Require students to write rhetorically. Elementary students are introduced to elements of rhetorical thinking when they begin to analyze texts for common structures such as compare and contrast, cause and effect, problem and solution, and so on. But rarely are they encouraged to use these structures in their own writing. These informational text structures form the core of rhetorical writing, which is really a method for presenting information in a logical and persuasive manner. It requires writers to organize their thinking into a recognizable form that leads the reader through a series of situations based on logical, ethical, or emotional arguments, and ends with a conclusion. All disciplines employ rhetorical writing forms. In geometry, for example, students write proofs based on a series of properties, theorems, and definitions. These often follow a prescribed format.

The use of sentence and paragraph frames (called *templates* by Graff & Birkenstein, 2006) can provide students with the language scaffolds they need to write academically. In a world history class, Kelly Crawford introduced the following paragraph frame for her students to use within a short paper on the effects of the Spanish Inquisition on the political decisions of the government. Paragraph frames such as this are not completed with single words, but rather with phrases and additional sentences. Her intent was not to provide the content, but rather to develop students' ability to explain an idea and support it with evidence.

The Spanish Inquisition had a profound effect on_____ because of _____. At the time, many people accepted this practice as _____. However, others opposed it. For example, _____. While the majority stood by because of fear of _____, a few protested. The result of this opposition was _____.

Video 6.2

Teacher
promotes
students'
reflection and
metacognition
after lesson.
*www.corwin.com/
rigorousreading*

In some cases, _____. Overall, the effect was _____. As historians have examined this era, they have noted that _____. One scholar, _____, wrote "_____" (Citation). Another historian, _____, said "_____" (Citation). In retrospect, the policy of _____, which supported the Inquisition, over time proved to be _____.

Ms. Crawford's students use frames like this to strengthen their ability to write rhetorically. By including specific frames that require students to quote from other texts, she further reinforces the use of primary source documents as a means for analyzing the content.

▶ Accessing Complex Texts Requires Students to Do Something After Reading

Let's assume that a group of students have read and discussed a piece of text with each other and their teacher. What should come next? Too often, the tasks that teachers assign after reading are unrelated to the reading itself. When students are not required to use information from the text in subsequent tasks, they often forget what they've read. Or worse, they learn that reading isn't that important and that they can complete the requirements for a class without really doing the readings.

Now imagine that three different classrooms have used the same piece of text, the "Declaration of Conscience" by Margaret Chase Smith (1950), which is a speech that was delivered to Congress criticizing national leadership and asking that the Senate reexamine the tactics used by the House Un-American Activities Committee and (without naming him) Senator Joe McCarthy. In one classroom, students are asked to provide examples from their lives for each of the "Four Horsemen of Calumny," namely, fear, ignorance, bigotry, and smear. In the second classroom, students are asked to apply the four principles of "Americanism" to specific events in history, namely, (1) the right to criticize, (2) the right to hold unpopular beliefs, (3) the right to protest, and (4) the right of independent thought. In the third classroom, students are asked to identify references to the U.S. Constitution in the Declaration of Conscience and to find the referenced sections, then summarize their findings and determine whether or not they agree with Smith's interpretation.

In thinking about each of these tasks, we must consider the ways in which students will use the texts that they have read in completing the task. The first task does not require that students have read the text; much less does it create a need to reread it. Students will be able to identify situations in which those words apply without ever looking at the text. The second task requires some understanding of the text under investigation and some thinking about specific events in history. The students will need to read some information to complete the task, but may not have to reread or produce evidence from Smith's text. The third task requires repeated readings of the text and the use of evidence from this text, and other texts, for completion. For that reason, it is more likely to communicate to students that reading is important and that they need to learn from what they read.

When a student offers an opinion or idea, the teacher or a peer should probe further by asking for evidence to substantiate the claim.

Types of Text-Dependent Tasks

There is a wide range of tasks that require students to read and understand a given text. We will highlight a few of them below, but anything that requires students to use what they have read is probably a good thing.

Perspective Writing

Many writers write to their teacher and consider him or her to be the audience, thereby missing the point of some writing tasks by failing to develop perspective and purpose in their writing. Santa and Havens (1995) developed the RAFT writing prompt to teach students to develop perspective in their writing. The prompt requires that students understand the Role, Audience, Format, and Topic for each piece of writing. For example, as part of a lesson on sportsmanship, physical educator Matt Thompson asked his students to respond to the following prompt after having read an article about the Olympics:

R   Bronze medal winner
A   Gold medal winner
F   Greeting card
T   Congratulations on your victory

Mr. Thompson knew that his students understood the lesson as he read paper after paper with complimentary notes and appropriate language. For example, Amber wrote:

Too often, the tasks that teachers assign after reading are unrelated to the reading itself.

Dear Winner!

I was so proud to be by your side when you crossed the line. You pushed me to be a better runner. Thank you for your encouragement. Of course I would have liked to win, but we had a fair race and we all did our best. Enjoy the title because you deserve it. I hope to see you again at the next race.

Until Next Time,
Amber

English teacher Marla Ramirez was not as satisfied with her students' understanding of a complex text—*The Metamorphosis* (Kafka, 1946), so she invited students to respond to the following prompt:

R Gregor Samsa
A Mr. and Mrs. Samsa, his parents
F Note
T Why don't you notice me?

Student after student focused on Gregor's literal struggle rather than his symbolic struggle for identity. For example, Manuel wrote:

My loving parents,

I am trying to turn over but I can't. I need your help. Please help me so that I can figure out how to live this way. I think that it is terrible that I am now a bug, but I am still your child. I need help to do things, so you should help me like when I was a kid.

Gregor

Ms. Ramirez understood that her students' writing reflected their literal understanding of the text, but not its metaphors, and that she needed to review some of the initial section of the book, as well as Kafka's purpose as a writer, if her students were going to be able to understand the existential message more deeply. After further instruction about the use of symbolism in the story, Manuel wrote a second response, using the same RAFT prompt:

Dear Mother and Father,

I have asked you for help, but you don't even notice that I need help. You have taken me for granted for all these years. I have been a good son to you. But you don't notice me when I am suffering. It is like I was just some lowly insect in your home, too small to be seen. If I did something unexpected, or something awful, would you see me then? Maybe for the first time? I feel like I am invisible to your eyes. Will you ever see me as a whole person, and not just the son you always count on and take for granted?

Gregor

Writing to Prompts

In addition to RAFT prompts, there are a number of other types of prompts that guide student thinking, require that they return to the text for evidence, and allow teachers to check for understanding (Fisher & Frey, 2012b), including the following:

- **Admit Slips:** On entering the classroom, students respond to an assigned topic such as, "Who was Napoleon and why should we care?" or "Describe the digestive process" or "Why are irrational numbers important in science and engineering?"

- **Crystal Ball:** Students describe what they think class will be about, what might happen next in the novel they're reading, or the next step in a science lab. For example, while reading a novel, the English teacher pauses and invites students to predict what the character will do next based on the information presented thus far.

- **Found Poems:** Students reread a piece of text, either something they have written or something published, and find key phrases. They arrange these into a free-verse poem structure without adding any new words.
- **Awards:** Students recommend someone or something for an award that the teacher has created such as "Most interesting character" or "Most dangerous chemical."
- **Yesterday's News:** Students summarize the information presented the day before, from a film, lecture, discussion, or reading. For example, after watching a video clip about the plague, students wrote a response to this type of prompt.
- **Take a Stand:** Students discuss their opinions about a controversial topic such as "What's worth fighting for?" in world history or "What is normal, anyway?" in psychology.
- **Letters:** Students write letters to others, including elected officials, family members, friends, or people who have made a difference. For example, students may respond to the prompt, "Write to Susan B. Anthony about the progress that has, or has not, been made related to individual rights."

Sentence frames can provide students with the language scaffolds they need to write academically.

In addition, when students respond to a specific writing prompt that requires that they use evidence from the text, the task becomes text dependent. However, it's not sufficient for students to simply include quotes from the text. They need to explain the quotes and integrate them in a thoughtful way. As Graff and Birkenstein (2006) note, "[T]he main problem with quotation arises when writers assume that the quotations speak for themselves" (p. 40). To address this, they provide a series of templates that writers can use to frame quotes. The evidence students use from the text needs to be *introduced,* perhaps with the following templates (p. 43):

- X states, "_____."
- In her book _____, X maintains that "_____."
- X disagrees when he writes, "_____."
- X complicates matters further when she writes, "_____."

Writers also have to *explain* the quotes that they have selected as evidence, perhaps with the following templates (p. 44):

- Basically, X is saying _____.
- In other words, X believes _____.
- In making this comment, X argues that _____.
- X's point is that _____.

Writers also need to show a *clear connection* to the surrounding text or a reason for including the quote within their own writing. For example,

- This is important because _____.
- This relates to _____.
- This contradicts _____ because _____.

Socratic Seminar

Socratic Seminar requires that students have read a text and are prepared to discuss it. There are four components of a Socratic Seminar:

1. **The text**, which should be selected because it is worthy of investigation and discussion
2. **The questions**, which should lead participants back to the text as they speculate, evaluate, define and clarify the issues involved
3. **The leader**—who can be a student or the teacher—who is both guide and participant, and helps participants clarify their position, involves reluctant participants, and restrains overactive members of the group
4. **The participants**, who come to the discussion having read the text, ready to share their ideas and perspectives with others

Socratic Seminars are not times when students simply espouse their own beliefs. They should be grounded in textual discussion. Students must consult the texts that are relevant to the discussion, or they will not be able to answer questions such as these:

- Could you give me an example or a metaphor to explain that?
- Can you find that in the text?
- Where does the reading support you?
- What are you assuming in that argument?

When students respond to a specific writing prompt that requires that they use evidence from the text, the task becomes text dependent.

Debates

Debates require that students carefully analyze texts such that they can make their case effectively. In a debate, students need to carefully examine an issue, research both sides of the issue, and be prepared to defend a position. As part of the debate process, students rely on texts for evidence. In preparing for debates, students read and reread several texts, taking notes that they can use later. During the debate, students use their resources to argue in a structured way. Of course, students have to understand the rules of a debate. Typically, a team debate has different phases, such as the following:

Pro—Someone presents the "for" position.

Con—Someone presents the "against" position.

Pro—Someone presents evidence related to the "for" position.

Con—Someone presents evidence related to the "against" position.

Pro—Someone refutes the evidence from the "against" position.

Con—Someone refutes the evidence from the "for" position.

Pro—Someone salvages the most persuasive arguments left and makes a concluding statement.

Con—Someone salvages the most persuasive arguments left and makes a concluding statement.

Typically, the judge reviews the proceedings and declares a debate winner. Figure 6.1 contains debate guidelines developed by high school English teacher Heather Anderson.

Moving Beyond the Text

Although it is important that many of the tasks students complete require that they read and reread the text, there are also times when the appropriate task requires students to move away from the text. Typically, these tasks come at the end of a unit of study and provide students with an opportunity to compare their learning and thinking across several texts or to make connections with their own experiences and beliefs. It is important to note that these extended tasks should be introduced only after students have deeply investigated a text and have a solid understanding of the information contained therein.

Socratic Seminar requires that students have read a text and are prepared to discuss it.

Video 6.3

Sample student debate.
www.corwin.com/ rigorousreading

Figure 6.1 Debate Guidelines

Each team will have at least two people on the affirmative (for) side and two people on the negative (against) side.

1. Affirmative (for) presents case: 3 minutes max
2. Negative (against) presents case: 3 minutes max
3. Affirmative (for) and negative (against) respond to one another: 4 minutes max
4. Affirmative (for) summarizes and concludes: 1 minutes max
5. Negative (against) summarizes and concludes: 1 minutes max

After the debate, the class will vote to see which side won. This vote will not influence your final grade.

Tips

1. **You are always right:** No matter what you really believe, if you want to win, then you have to know that whatever you say is correct and your opposition is always wrong.
2. **Strong central argument:** Every point you make should be linked back to this central argument.
3. **Rebut:** If the other side has an incorrect fact, rebut it. If they do not link back to their team's case, rebut it. If they give an example that has no relevance, rebut it. Remember, the opposition is always wrong.
4. **Never insult the opposition:** No matter how much you want to, don't! If you want to insult something, do it to their argument. Don't use personal attacks if you want to win.
5. **Have passion:** Believe in what you are saying and you probably will win. Speak from the heart, but also use logic and research.

Debate Sentence Frames

I will argue that . . .	I will show that . . .	You can see that . . .
The evidence shows that . . .	My opponent believes . . .	All the evidence points toward . . .
That is simply not true . . .	It is clear that . . .	My opponent is wrong because . . .

▶ Accessing Complex Texts Requires Formative Assessments

Internet searches often yield surprising results. Recently, Nancy searched one of her favorite sayings in preparation for a presentation she was doing about assessments: "You can't fatten sheep by weighing them." One of the results was an article from the April 1908 issue of the *Farm Journal* on early spring lambs. Among the advice to sheep farmers? Take care in apportioning their rations so as not to overfeed, provide healthy living conditions so they can grow, take careful measure of their progress, and keep this piece of wisdom in mind: "Study your sheep and know them not only as a flock but separately, and remember that they have an individuality as surely as your horse or cow" (Brick, 1908, p. 154).

Students are not sheep, of course, but our role as cultivators of young people has much in common with the role of a livestock farmer. As educators, we recognize the importance of a healthy learning climate, and we seek to create one each day. In addition, we apportion information so that students can act on their growing knowledge of the discipline. And we measure their progress throughout to see whether they are making expected gains. As part of effective practice, teachers routinely check for understanding through the learning process. This is most commonly accomplished by asking questions, analyzing tasks, and administering low-stakes quizzes to measure the extent to which students are acquiring new information and skills. But it's one thing to gather information (we're good at that); it's another to respond in meaningful ways and then plan for subsequent instruction. Without processes to provide students with solid feedback that yields deeper understanding, checking for understanding devolves into a game of "guess what's in the teacher's brain." And without ways to look for patterns across students, formative assessments become a frustrating academic exercise. Knowing both the flock and the individuals in it are the essential pieces of the puzzle for those in the cultivation business.

In debate, students rely on texts for evidence.

Knowing the Individual: Effective Feedback

Most of us have experienced poor feedback during our learning lives. The teacher who scrawled "rewrite this" in the margin of an essay we had written. The coach who told us, "No, you're doing it wrong, keep practicing." The coworker who took over the project and finished it for us when our progress stalled. The frustration on the learner's part matches that felt by the teacher, coach, or coworker: Why can't he or she get this? That mutual vexation produces a mutual sense of defeat. On the part of the learner, the internal dialogue becomes, "I can't do this." For the teacher, it's, "I can't teach this." Over time, blame sets in, and the student and teacher begin to find fault with each other.

Hattie and Timperley (2007) wrote about feedback across four dimensions: "Feedback about the task (FT), about the processing of the task (FP), about self-regulation (FR), and about the self as a person (FS)" (p. 90).

For example, "*You need to put a semicolon in this sentence*" (FT) has limited usefulness and is not usually generalized to other tasks.

On the other hand, "*Make sure that your sentences have noun-verb agreements because it's going make it easier for the reader to understand your argument*" (FP) gives feedback information about a writing convention necessary in all essays.

The researchers go on to note that feedback that moves from information about the process to information about self-regulation is the best of all. Such feedback might include something like the following: "*Try reading some of your sentences aloud so you can hear when you have and don't have noun-verb agreement.*"

The researchers go on to say that FS is the least useful ("*You're a good student*") even when it is positive in nature because it doesn't add anything to one's learning. A summary of the types of feedback can be found in Figure 6.2.

Done carefully, FT can have a modest amount of usefulness, as when editing a paper. Yet feedback about the task is by far the most common kind we offer. The problem is that the task-related feedback offers only endgame analysis and leaves the learner with little direction on what to do, particularly when there isn't any recourse to make changes. Most writing teachers will tell you that it is not uncommon for students to engage in limited revision, confined to the specific items listed in the teacher feedback—which then makes it more of an exercise in recopying than in revising. However, feedback about the processes used in the task, and further advice about

Although it is important that many of the tasks students complete require that they read and reread the text, there are also times when the appropriate task requires students to move away from the text.

Figure 6.2   Feedback Examples

Type	Example	Usefulness
Feedback about the task (FT)	"Make sure to change this from a period to an exclamation mark."	Limited
Feedback about the processing of the task (FP)	"You seem to want to emphasize this point. Be sure to use a strong verb to capture that intensity so your reader understands this as well."	Very useful
Feedback about self-regulation (FR)	"Read that passage aloud after you rewrite it to yourself to see if it matches the level of intensity you intend."	Very useful
Feedback about the self as a person (Fs)	"Good boy."	Not useful

the self-regulatory strategies one can use to make revisions, can leave the learner with a plan for next steps.

Consider the dialogue between English teacher John Goodwin and Alicia, a student in his class. Alicia has drafted an essay on bullying, and John is providing feedback about her work. Careful to frame his feedback so that it can result in a plan for revision, he draws her attention to her thesis statement and says, "It's helpful for writers to go back to the main point of the essay and read to see if the evidence is there. I highlight in yellow so I can see if I've done that." The two of them reread her first three paragraphs and highlight where she has provided national statistics and direct quotes from teachers she knows. "Now what I want you to do is to look for ways you've provided supporting evidence, like through citing sources. Let's highlight those in green." Alicia quickly notices that while she has made claims, she hasn't capitalized on any authoritative sources. As well, by confining her direct quotes to teachers at her school, she has limited the impact of her essay by failing to quote more widely known sources. The little bit of green on her essay illustrates what she needs to do next: strengthen her sources. "It sounds like you have a plan for revising the content. Let's meet again on Wednesday and you can update me on your progress."

As part of effective practice, teachers routinely check for understanding through the learning process.

Feedback of this nature takes a few minutes yet can add up quickly in a crowded classroom. For this reason, many teachers rely on written forms of feedback as a substitute for direct conversations. Even when providing feedback in written form, the guidelines described above remain the same: Focus on the processes needed for the task, move to information about behaviors that are within the student's influence to change, and steer clear of comments that are either too global or too minute to be of much use. Wiggins (1998) advises constructing written feedback so that it meets four important criteria. First, it must be timely so that it is paired as closely as possible with the attempt; second, it should be specific in nature; third, it should be written in a manner that it understandable to the student; and fourth, it should be actionable so that the learner can make revisions.

Knowing the Flock: Feed-Forward

While feedback is primarily offered at the individual level, the concept of *feeding-up* refers to the process of making instructional decisions about what should happen next for the class as a whole (Frey & Fisher, 2011). Data about student progress are commonly gathered using common formative assessments that are either commercially produced or teacher-made. In addition, many school teams engage in consensus scoring with colleagues to calibrate assessment practices, especially those associated with tasks that have a significant qualitative component, such as writing (Fisher, Frey, Farnan, Fearn, & Petersen, 2004). However, consensus scoring requires time for colleagues to work together—something that can be hard to come by and can therefore be a limitation to these practices. The good news is that one's own classroom can also serve as the unit of analysis for formative assessment.

With all of the solid feedback provided to students, it seems natural to take this one step further by recording results and doing some pattern analysis. For example, second-grade teacher Elena Vitsen conferred with students during their independent reading to check on their progress toward informational reading standard 5, analyzing text structures. "I've been working with them on how we use images, captions, and subheadings to scan and locate information in texts," she explained. "I've been checking in with them about using their science textbook this way."

She selects an unfamiliar passage from the book and asks questions about the content of the caption and image, as well as its relation to the main portion of the text. "I'm especially interested right now in whether they are able to accurately predict the content of the passage and figure out where the image belongs," she said. Her error analysis sheet is in Figure 6.3.

Unlike a checklist to track mastery, this error analysis sheet is used to identify and highlight those who are struggling. She logs the initials of students who are still having difficulty with major concepts despite initial instruction, then makes decisions about follow-up and reteaching. For example, the error analysis sheet showed her that almost the entire class was still having difficulty relating the visual to the correct passage. That tells her that reteaching to the whole group is in order. On the other hand, smaller groups of students were having trouble with other concepts.

> I was surprised that I still had a few who aren't using bold words effectively. We've had lots of experiences with these, and I thought everyone had it. I'll need to pull those students into a small group, because the majority of the class is doing fine otherwise.

She will plan further scaffolded instruction for these small groups.

Seventh-grade humanities teacher Cory Laughlin is also concerned with examining his students' progress toward informational reading anchor standard 5. "They're writing longer research papers now, but they haven't been applying much in the way of formal and logical organization to their own work, even though we read articles that use these methods," he said. He decided to require students to include some structural analysis of the texts they were reading. "We started with some more obvious ones, such as opinion pieces with titles that included phrases like 'Pros and Cons,'"

It's one thing to gather information (we're good at that); it's another to respond in meaningful ways and then plan for subsequent instruction.

Video 6.4

Daily checks for understanding help teachers identify instructional needs.
www.corwin.com/ rigorousreading

Video 6.5

A teacher discusses his use of error analysis.
www.corwin.com/ rigorousreading

Figure 6.3	Grade 2 Error Analysis of Anchor Standard 5 Related to Informational Text

Task	Initials of Students Who Are Having Difficulty With This Skill
Locates caption	
Reads caption and relates it to the text	
Reads caption and relates it to the visual information	
Locates bold word	
Describes the role of bold words	
Finds meaning of bold word using glossary	
Locates subheading	
Describes content expected in the section based on the subheading	
Identifies appropriate visual/graphic and caption related to the text in a subheading	

he said. "As we did close readings, I made sure to spend time on the structures the writer used, and how he laid out his argument." His students read several articles about a bill being debated in the state legislature about granting amnesty to people who witnessed a drug overdose and called 911. In addition to completing the précis writing, his students analyzed the degree to which each writer organized his or her argument sufficiently such that a reader could logically follow the text. "This has been tough for them to do, because they're so sure that if something's published it must automatically be well written." Mr. Laughlin adds the initials of the students in each period who are still struggling with this, so that he can follow up with them.

> They'll need some more scaffolded reading instruction, but it's not like the whole class does. My problem is that I see 180 kids a day, and it gets hard to remember who needs more teaching. Keeping track lets me see who should be in a needs-based group.

Mr. Laughlin's error analysis sheet is in Figure 6.4.

▶ Summary

We are changed by text. We use complex texts to bring the world into our classrooms. But students' potential for learning remains untapped until we provide them with culminating assessments that are equally as complex as the texts they are reading. The texts you choose should serve as a platform for extending ideas and building curiosity. The use of writing, debates and discussions, and Socratic Seminars provides students with the chance to fully integrate texts into their view of the world.

These culminating tasks are never truly final, as we learn more about our students—including what they know and don't yet know—through careful observation. What we hear them say during discussion, or read in their writing, sparks further understanding about what should come next. In this way, student assessment never ends until the very last day of school. Caring teachers apply what they have learned about their students to future instruction. They use feedback in ways that build student understanding,

Video 6.6

Teacher reteaches students to use evidence after the error analysis revealed a need.
www.corwin.com/ rigorousreading

Figure 6.4	Grade 7 Error Analysis of Anchor Standard 5 Related to Informational Text

Task	Initials of Students Who Did Not Demonstrate This Skill				
	Period 1	Period 2	Period 3	Period 4	Period 5
Names appropriate text structure					
Identifies evidence from the text to support the structure					
Discusses the development of ideas related to the structure					
Notes signal words that are consistent with the structure					
Describes one section of the text and its relationship with the information presented					
Describes a second section of the text and its relationship with the information presented					

Nancy leads a
group of teachers
in a data review.
*www.corwin.com/
rigorousreading*

and they look for the patterns that will inform their next instructional moves. It is much in the manner of the sheep tender looking over the flock. According to Brick (1908),

> The man who does not like sheep, and who is not willing to devote lots of time to their care . . . has no business meddling with the Spring Lamb . . . To be successful, he must also be gentle, with a watchful eye for little things . . . and a hundred minor details upon which success depends. (p. 154)

In short, the tender must also heed the warning Brick delivered almost a century ago: "You can't fatten sheep by weighing them." In the same way, it is through nurturing and feeding our students—and not merely through measuring them—that we provide them with a window through which they can see the world and themselves in the words of others.

Coda

We have come to the end of this book with just a few words left before you close the cover. You have read this book because you care deeply about your craft and your students. We applaud you for that. You know that simply assigning students complex texts and then wishing them well is not going to yield breakthrough results. You also know that teaching is more than test scores. Yes, providing students access to complex texts will improve their achievement on the next generation of assessments. But more than that, accessing complex texts invites students into the scholarly world. This may sound like hyperbole, but we really believe that unlocking complex texts is the most important thing a teacher can do for his or her students. And now that you have read this book, you have the keys in your hands. The access points in this book work. They ensure that students have the experiences, instruction, and support necessary to read and understand the wide range of texts they will encounter throughout their lives.

Professional Learning Guide

Rigorous Reading: 5 Access Points for Comprehending Complex Texts

Introduction
and Purpose

Introduction

This Professional Learning Guide offers a framework for professional development to support K–12 teachers in guiding and instructing all students in the comprehension of complex texts. While this guide is intended for school site professional developers to use with teachers, it may also be used by literacy coaches, in grade-level or cross-grade-level study groups, in professional learning communities, or by administrators and district leaders of professional development. Individual teachers who are seeking to further their professional development may also use this guide to enhance their skills and knowledge in teaching students, K–12, how to gain access to complex texts.

Purpose of *Rigorous Reading: 5 Access Points for Comprehending Complex Texts*

In this guide, the goal of Nancy Frey and Doug Fisher is to offer educators research-based literacy instruction to support all students, K–12, in achieving proficient understanding of complex texts based on the *gradual release of responsibility* framework through five access points:

1. Purpose and Modeling

2. Close and Scaffolded Reading Instruction

3. Collaborative Conversations

4. An Independent Reading Staircase

5. Demonstrating Understanding and Assessing Performance

With a shared vision and goals, educators can collaborate with one another to deliver clear and purposeful instruction that provides students, K–12, with opportunities to become highly effective in reading complex texts. These five access points provide teachers with strong literacy instruction addressing the Anchor Standards 1 and 10 in the Common Core State Standards.

Module Sessions

Approximate completion times for each module are provided within this guide; however, times may vary based on the needs, collaboration style, and interaction of your group. Additionally, modules vary in length. They may be combined in several all-day workshops or presented over a series of shorter sessions to suit your needs. All modules are organized with the following headings:

- Materials You Will Need
- Segment Outlines
- Wrap Up
- Supplementary Sessions

Supplementary Sessions are provided as an extension for participants who would like to enhance their professional development, deepen their knowledge, or enrich a dialogue.

Materials for Sessions

In the "Materials You Will Need" sections of the sessions you will find references to the following:

Video clips: We suggest using the existing Frey and Fisher classroom video clips and recommend specific clips for use during each session. You can access these via the QR codes that are located in this book. They are also housed on the companion website at **www.corwin.com/rigorousreading.** If you have similar or relevant videos familiar to your group, please feel free to include them as well if it will support the effectiveness and improvement of your group's instructional practice.

PowerPoint slides: These are available at **www.corwin.com/rigorousreading.**

Copies of figures: The figures referenced are located in this book. You can also print them out from **www.corwin.com/rigorousreading.**

Ramping Up for Complex Texts

▶ **Estimated Time: 1 Hour 15 Minutes**

The purpose of this module is to understand and examine text complexity and close reading in relation to Reading Anchor Standard 1 and Anchor Standard 10. Teachers will examine Anchor Standard 10, gaining knowledge and know-how in text analysis by learning how to identify and evaluate the three elements involved in determining text complexity: quantitative evaluation, qualitative evaluation, and matching readers with texts and tasks. Furthermore, teachers will recognize the importance of the framework of *gradual release of responsibility* (e.g., Fisher & Frey, 2008; Pearson & Fielding, 1991), and its impact on students with access to complex texts. This module builds the foundational knowledge for the subsequent five modules. Spending quality-focused time during this first module will greatly enrich the effectiveness of further sessions.

Materials You Will Need

1. Highlighters

2. **PowerPoint Slides 1.1–1.12**

3. Copies of **Figure 1.1:** Anchor Standard 10: Read and comprehend complex literary and informational texts independently and proficiently

4. Copies of **Figure 1.3:** Anchor Standard 1: Read closely to determine what the text says explicitly and to make logical inferences from it; cite specific textual evidence when writing or speaking to support conclusions drawn from the text

5. Qualitative Measures for Text Complexity Rubric (Supplementary Session), pages 47–48 in *Text Complexity: Raising Rigor in Reading* by Doug Fisher, Nancy Frey, and Diane Lapp

6. Videos

   a. **Video 1.1:** "Doug discusses text complexity."

   b. **Video 1.2:** "Nancy reviews a text for the factors of complexity."

   c. **Video 1.3**: "Doug discusses close reading."

   d. **Video 1.4:** "Teacher modeling comprehension strategies."

   e. **Video 1.5**: "Doug talks about the gradual release of responsibility."

▶ Segment I: Approximately 10 Minutes
Stating the Purpose of This Session

a. Have participants read pages 1–3 of Chapter 1 in *Rigorous Reading*, which describe Doug and Nancy's personal experiences with complex texts that included too much or too little scaffolded instruction.

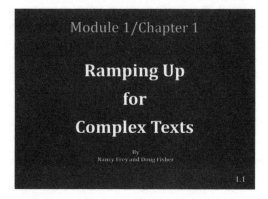

b. After reading, have participants turn and talk: Why and *how* can either type of experience affect students' ability to access complex texts?

c. Project **PowerPoint Slide 1.2.** Ask for volunteers to share responses with the whole group.

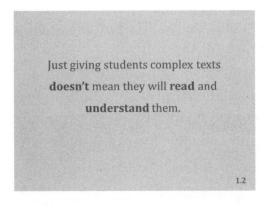

d. Project **PowerPoint Slide 1.3.** Sum up this introduction time by stating how intentional instruction is scaffolded instruction; that is, it is knowing when to transfer the cognitive and metacognitive responsibility to students, and reconsidering the types of texts and their purpose for instruction.

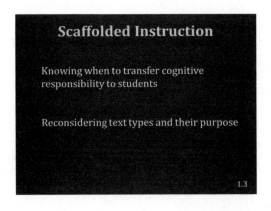

▶ Segment II: Approximately 10 Minutes

Examine the Learning Progressions of Anchor Standard 10: Read and Comprehend Complex Literary and Informational Texts Independently and Proficiently

a. Project **PowerPoint Slide 1.4:** Directions for Examining Learning Progressions of Anchor Standard 10, or provide participants with a copy.

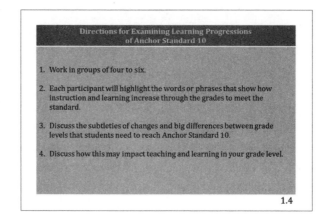

b. Pass out copies of **Figure 1.1:** Anchor Standard 10: Read and comprehend complex literary and informational texts independently and proficiently.

c. In groups of four to six, vertical or grade level, have participants identify and highlight on their copies the learning progressions: What is added to the standard for each next grade level, K–12, for Anchor Standard 10?

d. If you wish, project **PowerPoint Slide 1.5** as an example. Note that kindergarten is highlighted completely since the standard begins here and is new for this grade.

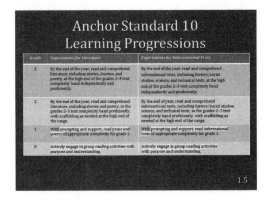

Anchor Standard 10
Learning Progressions

Grade	Expectations for Literature	Expectations for Informational Texts
3	By the end of the year, read and comprehend literature, including stories, dramas, and poetry, at the high end of the grades 2–3 text complexity band independently and proficiently.	By the end of the year, read and comprehend informational texts, including history/social studies, science, and technical texts, at the high end of the grades 2–3 text complexity band independently and proficiently.
2	By the end of the year, read and comprehend literature, including stories and poetry, in the grades 2–3 text complexity band proficiently, with scaffolding as needed at the high end of the range.	By the end of year, read and comprehend informational texts, including history/social studies, science, and technical texts, in the grades 2–3 text complexity band proficiently, with scaffolding as needed at the high end of the range.
1	With prompting and support, read prose and poetry of appropriate complexity for grade 1.	With prompting and support, read informational texts of appropriate complexity for grade 1.
K	Actively engage in group reading activities with purpose and understanding.	Actively engage in group reading activities with purpose and understanding.

1.5

e. Discuss the subtleties of the changes and the big differences between grade levels in Anchor Standard 10. How might teaching and learning be affected?

f. Have groups reflect on new concepts and skills that are introduced at their grade level. Reflect on the importance of meeting Anchor Standard 10.

Figure 1.1 Anchor Standard 10: Read and comprehend complex literary and informational texts independently and proficiently.

Grade	Expectations for Literature	Expectations for Informational Texts
12	By the end of grade 12, read and comprehend literature, including stories, dramas, and poems, at the high end of the grades 11–CCR text complexity band independently and proficiently.	By the end of grade 12, read and comprehend literary nonfiction at the high end of the grades 11–CCR text complexity band independently and proficiently.
11	By the end of grade 11, read and comprehend literature, including stories, dramas, and poems, in the grades 11–CCR text complexity band proficiently, with scaffolding as needed at the high end of the range.	By the end of grade 11, read and comprehend literary nonfiction in the grades 11–CCR text complexity band proficiently, with scaffolding as needed at the high end of the range.
10	By the end of grade 10, read and comprehend literature, including stories, dramas, and poems, at the high end of the grades 9–10 text complexity band independently and proficiently.	By the end of grade 10, read and comprehend literary nonfiction at the high end of the grades 9–10 text complexity band independently and proficiently.
9	By the end of grade 9, read and comprehend literature, including stories, dramas, and poems, in the grades 9–10 text complexity band proficiently, with scaffolding as needed at the high end of the range.	By the end of grade 9, read and comprehend literary nonfiction in the grades 9–10 text complexity band proficiently, with scaffolding as needed at the high end of the range.
8	By the end of the year, read and comprehend literature, including stories, dramas, and poems, at the high end of grades 6–8 text complexity band independently and proficiently.	By the end of the year, read and comprehend literary nonfiction at the high end of the grades 6–8 text complexity band independently and proficiently.
7	By the end of the year, read and comprehend literature, including stories, dramas, and poems, in the grades 6–8 text complexity band proficiently, with scaffolding as needed at the high end of the range.	By the end of the year, read and comprehend literary nonfiction in the grades 6–8 text complexity band proficiently, with scaffolding as needed at the high end of the range.
6	By the end of the year, read and comprehend literature, including stories, dramas, and poems, in the grades 6–8 text complexity band proficiently, with scaffolding as needed at the high end of the range.	By the end of the year, read and comprehend literary nonfiction in the grades 6–8 text complexity band proficiently, with scaffolding as needed at the high end of the range.

Grade	Expectations for Literature	Expectations for Informational Texts
5	By the end of the year, read and comprehend literature, including stories, dramas, and poetry, at the high end of the grades 4–5 text complexity band independently and proficiently.	By the end of the year, read and comprehend informational texts, including history/social studies, science, and technical texts, at the high end of the grades 4–5 text complexity band independently and proficiently.
4	By the end of the year, read and comprehend literature, including stories, dramas, and poetry, in the grades 4–5 text complexity band proficiently, with scaffolding as needed at the high end of the range.	By the end of year, read and comprehend informational texts, including history/social studies, science, and technical texts, in the grades 4–5 text complexity band proficiently, with scaffolding as needed at the high end of the range.
3	By the end of the year, read and comprehend literature, including stories, dramas, and poetry, at the high end of the grades 2–3 text complexity band independently and proficiently.	By the end of the year, read and comprehend informational texts, including history/social studies, science, and technical texts, at the high end of the grades 2–3 text complexity band independently and proficiently.
2	By the end of the year, read and comprehend literature, including stories and poetry, in the grades 2–3 text complexity band proficiently, with scaffolding as needed at the high end of the range.	By the end of year, read and comprehend informational texts, including history/social studies, science, and technical texts, in the grades 2–3 text complexity band proficiently, with scaffolding as needed at the high end of the range.
1	With prompting and support, read prose and poetry of appropriate complexity for grade 1.	With prompting and support, read informational texts appropriately complex for grade 1.
K	Actively engage in group reading activities with purpose and understanding.	Actively engage in group reading activities with purpose and understanding.

▶ Segment III: Approximately 30 Minutes
The Three Elements of Text Complexity

a. Watch **Video 1.1:** "Doug discusses text complexity."

b. After viewing, project **PowerPoint Slide 1.6 and Slide 1.7**. Have your participants split into groups of three to examine the three elements of text complexity: quantitative evaluation, qualitative evaluation, and reader and task considerations.

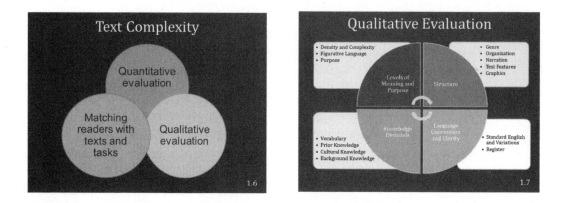

c. Project **PowerPoint Slide 1.8:** Directions for Jigsaw Activity for Three Elements of Text Complexity, or provide participants with a copy.

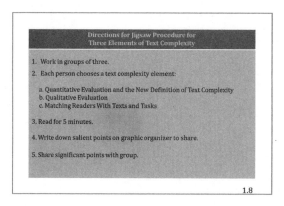

d. Have each person within a group choose a different element of text complexity and read the corresponding section from Chapter 1 of *Rigorous Reading*. Have them take notes of the salient points to share with the other group members. (Note: You may want to have the participant who is reading the quantitative evaluation section also read starting from the subheading A New Definition of Text Complexity, as this section provides additional information for quantitative evaluation.)

e. Have the groups conduct a jigsaw discussion of the three elements of text complexity.

f. Watch **Video 1.2:** "Nancy reviews a text for the factors of complexity."

▶ Segment IV: Approximately 10 Minutes
Examining the Learning Progressions of Anchor Standard 1: Reading Closely

a. Project **PowerPoint Slide 1.9**: Directions for Examining Learning Progressions of Anchor Standard 1, or provide participants with a copy.

b. Pass out copies of **Figure 1.3:** Anchor Standard 1: Read closely to determine what the text says explicitly and to make logical inferences from it; cite specific textual evidence when writing or speaking to support conclusions drawn from the text.

c. In groups of four to six, vertical or grade level, have participants identify the learning progressions: What is added for each next grade level, K–12, for Anchor Standard 1?

d. Highlight the words or phrases that show how instruction and learning increase through the grades to meet the standard. Kindergarten is highlighted completely since the standard begins here and is new for this grade.

e. Discuss the subtleties of the changes and the big differences between grade levels in Anchor Standard 1. How might teaching and learning be affected?

f. Have groups reflect on new concepts and skills that are introduced at their grade level. Reflect on the importance of meeting Anchor Standard 1.

Figure 1.3 Anchor Standard 1: Read closely to determine what the text says explicitly and to make logical inferences from it; cite specific textual evidence when writing or speaking to support conclusions drawn from the text.

Grades	Expectations for Literature and Informational Texts
11–12	Cite strong and thorough textual evidence to support analysis of what the text says explicitly as well as inferences drawn from the text, including determining where the text leaves matters uncertain.
9–10	Cite strong and thorough textual evidence to support analysis of what the text says explicitly as well as inferences drawn from the text.
8	Cite the textual evidence that most strongly supports an analysis of what the text says explicitly as well as inferences drawn from the text.
7	Cite several pieces of textual evidence to support analysis of what the text says explicitly as well as inferences drawn from the text.
6	Cite textual evidence to support analysis of what the text says explicitly as well as inferences drawn from the text.
5	Quote accurately from a text when explaining what the text says explicitly and when drawing inferences from the text.
4	Refer to details and examples in a text when explaining what the text says explicitly and when drawing inferences from the text.
3	Ask and answer questions to demonstrate understanding of a text, referring explicitly to the text as the basis for the answers.
2	Ask and answer such questions as who, what, where, when, why, and how to demonstrate understanding of key details in a text.
1	Ask and answer questions about key details in a text.
K	With prompting and support, ask and answer questions about key details in a text.

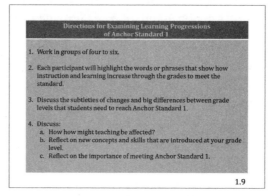

Directions for Examining Learning Progressions of Anchor Standard 1

1. Work in groups of four to six.

2. Each participant will highlight the words or phrases that show how instruction and learning increase through the grades to meet the standard.

3. Discuss the subtleties of changes and big differences between grade levels that students need to reach Anchor Standard 1.

4. Discuss:
   a. How how might teaching be affected?
   b. Reflect on new concepts and skills that are introduced at your grade level.
   c. Reflect on the importance of meeting Anchor Standard 1.

1.9

▶ Segment V: Approximately 10 Minutes
An Introduction to Close Reading

a. Watch and discuss **Video 1.3**: "Doug discusses close reading."

b. Turn and talk to cover significant points relevant to a close read.

c. Project **PowerPoint Slide 1.10** to highlight the following:
   i. Intention
   ii. Foster critical-thinking skills for deeper comprehension
   iii. Begin in kindergarten
   iv. Assumption-worthy text

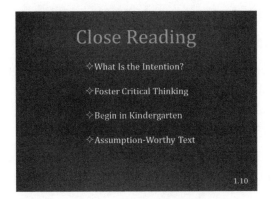

d. Inform participants that in Chapter 3, and in Module 3 Segments III and IV, close reading will be discussed in further detail.

▶ Segment VI: Approximately 10 Minutes

The Importance of Comprehension Strategies Instruction for Accessing Complex Texts

a. Have participants generate a list of the types of comprehension strategies they currently use and how they currently use them.

b. Use **PowerPoint Slide 1.11** to discuss the comprehension strategies and the pathway they provide for accessing complex texts.

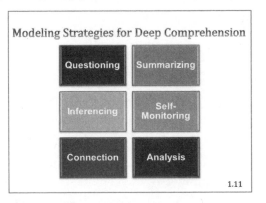

c. Watch **Video 1.4:** "Teacher modeling comprehension strategies." Have participants look for the type of comprehension strategies the teacher is using and the reasons he or she is using a specific strategy.

d. Remind participants of the danger of teaching comprehension strategies in isolation because it may interfere with deep comprehension (see text pages 17–18 for more information and quote).

▶ Segment VII: Approximately 10 Minutes
The Gradual Release of Responsibility

a. Watch **Video 1.5:** "Doug talks about the gradual release of responsibility."

b. Discuss significant points and implications for accessing complex texts with a partner.

c. Discuss how this framework builds and provides for purposeful intentional instruction for students to access complex texts.

▶ Wrap Up: Approximately 5 Minutes
One Final Note

Inform participants how the next sessions will build on the five access points from the text. Share the titles and brief descriptions from **PowerPoint Slide 1.12:**

- Access Point One: Purpose and Modeling
- Access Point Two: Close and Scaffolded Reading Instruction
- Access Point Three: Collaborative Conversations
- Access Point Four: An Independent Reading Staircase
- Access Point Five: Demonstrating Understanding and Assessing Performance

▶ Supplementary Segments

a. **Analyzing texts.** In follow-up sessions, such as those for specific grade levels, have teachers use the Qualitative Measures Rubric of Text Complexity Rubric on page 47 and 48 in *Text Complexity: Raising Rigor in Reading* by Doug Fisher, Nancy Frey, and Diane Lapp.

b. Supply student texts or have teachers bring texts they have used previously for instruction.

c. Begin with quantitative evaluation. Then project **PowerPoint Slide 1.7** and use the rubric to evaluate the qualitative aspects of the text. If the texts are suitable, make a note of the list of factors that support the four broad levels of complexity highlighted on the rubric: levels of meaning and purpose, structure, language conventionality and purpose, and knowledge demands.

d. If texts evaluated are not appropriate for the teachers' grade level, give those texts to another, more appropriate grade level, as these texts may have no purposeful intention to support students in deeper comprehension.

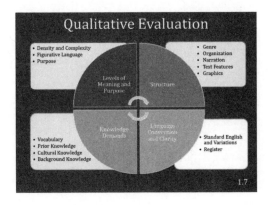

References

Fisher, D., & Frey, N. (2008). *Better learning for structured teaching: A framework for the gradual release of responsibility.* Alexandria, VA: ASCD.

Pearson, P. D., & Fielding, L. (1991). Comprehension instruction. In R. Barr, M. L. Kamil, P. Mosenthal, & P. D. Pearson (Eds.), *Handbook of reading research* (Vol. 2, pp. 815–860). Mahwah, NJ: Erlbaum.

Access Point One

Purpose and Modeling

▶ **Estimated Time: 2 Hours**

The purpose of this module is to help participants understand the importance, key principles, and indicators of modeling how to read complex texts through think-alouds, demonstrations, and annotation. Additionally, participants will identify the characteristics of a quality purpose statement and will understand how a quality purpose statement will both engage students and support them in accessing complex texts and completing assigned tasks.

Materials You Will Need

1. Copies of **Figure 2.1:** Planning for Purpose and Modeling

2. **PowerPoint Slides 2.1–2.10**

3. Poster paper, markers and tape, if needed, for Segment III **Examining the Five Principles of Modeling**

4. Videos

a. **Video 2.1**: "A teacher models for her students."

b. **Video 2.2**: "An elementary teacher models word solving."

c. **Video 2.3**: "A high school teacher models word solving."

d. **Video 2.4**: "A collection of purpose statements in elementary classrooms."

e. **Video 2.5**: "A collection of purpose statements in secondary classrooms."

f. **Video 2.6**: "Making sure students know the purpose."

g. **Video 2.7**: "Complex texts and standards" (optional for supplementary sessions).

▶ Segment I: Approximately 3 Minutes
Stating the Purpose of This Session

a. If you wish, project **PowerPoint Slide 2.1** to begin Segment I.

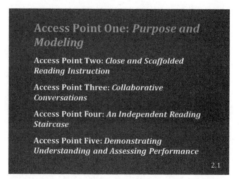

b. Project **PowerPoint Slide 2.2.**

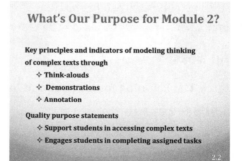

c. State the purpose of this module for participants:

    i. To understand the importance, key principles, and indicators of modeling for students—through think-alouds, demonstrations, and annotation—how to read and comprehend complex texts.

    ii. Identify the characteristics of a quality purpose statement and understand how a quality purpose statement will both engage students and support them in accessing complex texts and completing assigned tasks.

▶ Segment II: Approximately 15 Minutes
Modeling: How to Access Complex Texts

a. If participants have not previously read Chapter 2, have them read the Introduction and Accessing Complex Texts Requires Modeling sections now.

b. Tell participants they are going to watch a teacher modeling in the classroom. Use **Video 2.1:** "A teacher models for her students."

c. Have participants write down their observations of the modeling the teacher does for her students. What are the ways the teacher modeled her thinking about a complex text for the students?

d. After the video, have participants turn and talk with a partner regarding the types of modeling that they observed in the lesson. Share a few responses with the whole group.

e. Ask the group: *Why* is it important to model for students *how* to access complex texts? Summarize the following points **(PowerPoint Slide 2.3)** if they do not come up in the discussion:

    i. Complex texts demand more from readers than readings that are a comfortable and an appropriate match.

    ii. There is a difference between how expert and novice readers approach complex texts: novice readers often give up or approach all texts in the same manner.

    iii. Modeling allows the teacher to clarify comprehension problems, to highlight predicted areas of difficulty, and to show how an expert reader interacts with a complex text.

iv. Modeling demonstrates the habits of active readers

v. Modeling demonstrates persistence and a willingness to read a difficult text because it is worth it.

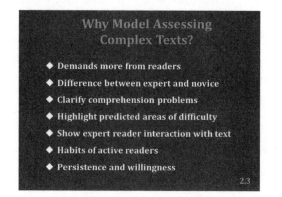

▶ Segment III: Approximately 60 Minutes
Examining the Five Principles of Modeling

a. In teams of five, participants examine the five principles and methods for modeling through a small-group teamwork presentation.

b. If you wish, project **PowerPoint Slide 2.4:** Directions for Examining Five Principles and Methods for Modeling, or provide participants with a copy of these instructions.

c. Have participants count off, starting with 1 and ending with 5, and repeating this procedure until all participants are assigned a number from 1 to 5. All participants who are number 1 form a group, number 2s form a group, and so on until you have five groups (Note: If you have a large group and the teams have more than five members, you may want split up to form more than one team).

d. Assign each group a principle to examine:

i. Model that which is difficult for students

ii. Model ways to resolve problems

iii. Model how you interact with text

iv. Model through think-alouds

v. Model through interactive shared readings

e. Each team prepares a short 5–10 minute presentation on the elements and the methods of that particular principle.

f. After each principle is presented, provide additional key points not mentioned in presentations.

g. After presentation(s) of Principle 2: Model ways to resolve problems, watch one of the following videos depending on grade levels taught by your participants (or use both if you have a mix of grade levels and staff): **Video 2.2:** "An elementary teacher models word solving"; **Video 2.3:** "A high school teacher models word solving."

h. If you wish, project **PowerPoint Slide 2.5.** After viewing the video, discuss the relationship between Common Core State Standards and the importance of using context clues, word parts or morphology, and other resources to uncover the meaning of unknown words.

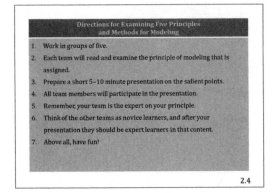

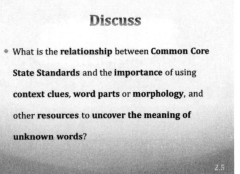

▶ Segment IV: Approximately 2 Minutes
Key Points of Modeling How to Read Complex Texts

a. If you wish, project **PowerPoint Slide 2.6:** Key Points of Modeling.

b. Recap for participants the key points of modeling how to read complex texts:

i. Students may develop habits that they will use independently.

ii. Modeling is often accompanied by a think-aloud that consistently contains "I" statements to invite the learner into the mind of the teacher.

iii. Modeling provides students with examples, not formulas, which they can follow while they complete their own work.

iv. Annotating the text while reading is a crucial in order to closely read complex texts.

v. Teachers should model their use of resources and model the appropriate ways to ask other people for help.

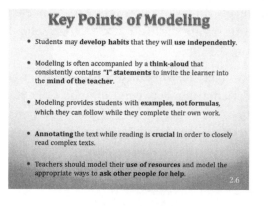

▶ Segment V: Approximately 2 Minutes
Significance of Quality Purpose Statements

If you wish, project **PowerPoint Slide 2.7:** Quality Purpose Statements

a. Impart to participants the four significant goals of a Quality Purpose Statement:

b. Inform students what they will learn and ways in which they may show or explain their comprehension.

c. Support the teacher in lesson planning, so student assignments and tasks are in alignment with the expected learning outcomes.

d. Drive instruction, differentiation, and assessment.

e. Create the foundation of quality lesson planning and instructional delivery.

▶ Segment VI: Approximately 20 Minutes
Identifying the Components of Quality Purpose Statements

a. Discuss with the participants the two components of purpose statements: content and language. If you wish, project **PowerPoint Slide 2.8**.

  i. Content—Content standards help alignment for high expectations; however, they should not be used in isolation.

  ii. Language—This refers to the function and structure of the purpose statement: the words we choose to describe how students will demonstrate or express their learning.

b. View **Video 2.4**: "A collection of purpose statements in elementary classrooms," or **Video 2.5**: "A collection of purpose statements in secondary classrooms."

c. While viewing the video, have participants take notes on the type of language and the content the teachers use in their purpose statements.

d. After the video, have participants turn and talk with a colleague about what they noticed in terms of the content and language the teachers used in their purpose statements.

e. Share a few comments with the whole group.

▶ Segment VII: Approximately 15 Minutes
Making Sure Students Know the Purpose

a. Watch **Video 2.6:** "Making sure students know the purpose." Have participants focus on how the teacher in the video ensures the students know the purpose of the lesson

b. After the video, Project **PowerPoint Slide 2.9.** Discuss with the whole group what the teacher in the video did to ensure the students recognized the purpose of the lesson.

   i. "What does she say or do so students know the purpose of the lesson?"

   ii. "How does the teacher know the students know the purpose of the lesson?"

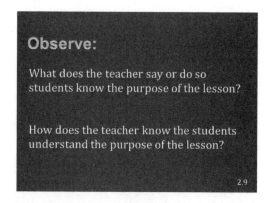

Observe:

What does the teacher say or do so students know the purpose of the lesson?

How does the teacher know the students understand the purpose of the lesson?

2.9

▶ Wrap Up: Approximately 3 Minutes
One Final Note

a. Summarize two noteworthy points for Access Point One: Purpose and Modeling. If you wish, project **PowerPoint Slide 2.10:** One Final Note.

   i. Creating and stating a clear purpose statement set a very strong foundation and structure for an effective and relevant lesson.

ii. When students are given access to how you, as an expert reader, solve comprehension problems through explicit modeling and annotation, they can then apply these practices during their own independent reading.

b. Announce next session—Access Point Two: Close and Scaffolded Reading Instruction.

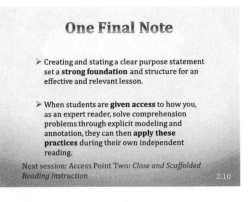

▶ Supplementary Session(s): Approximately 30 Minutes
Planning for Complex Texts

In follow-up session(s) such as with teachers of specific grade levels, have teachers use **Figure 2.1:** Planning for Purpose and Modeling.

a. Supply complex texts for specific grade levels or have teachers bring complex texts they have used previously for instruction.

b. Participants will work in groups of two or three to develop lessons for complex texts with a focus on Purpose and Modeling.

c. Have participants teach the lesson(s) to their classes. Plan a time to meet, discuss, and reflect on the lesson(s) in further sessions.

Figure 2.1   Planning for Purpose and Modeling

Assessed Need: I have noticed that the students in my classroom need to work on:

Standards:

Text I will use:

Materials needed for this lesson are:

Purpose of the lesson is:

Model
- Parts to emphasize

Figure 2.1   (Continued)

Scaffold
- Questions to ask

Assess
- These are the students who need extra support

Practice
- Students will practice using the strategy or skill during

Reflection
- What did I notice about what my students understood?

- What did I notice about my students' misunderstandings?

Access Point Two

Close and Scaffolded Reading Instruction

▶ **Estimated Time: 3.5 Hours**

The purpose of Module 3 is for participants to identify and understand the six essential practices of close reading instruction. Additionally, they will understand the importance of the six categories of text-based questions, which are paramount to close reading instruction. Participants will also comprehend the Four Principles of Scaffolded Instruction and understand how questions and prompts are fundamental to the practice of scaffolded instruction. These principles and practices will help participants gain a thorough understanding of these two instructional practices, close and scaffolded reading, and how they are avenues to support students as they begin to take responsibility for their learning, and become analytic readers.

Materials You Will Need

1. Copies of **Four Principles of Scaffolded Reading Instruction Graphic Organizer** and **Text-Dependent Questions Template** for Supplementary Session

2. Copies of **Figure 3.2:** Text-Dependent Questions, **Figure 3.3:** Sample Text-Dependent Questions, **Figure 3.4:** Types of Prompts, and **Figure 3.5:** Types of Cues (if participants do not have *Rigorous Reading* with them).

3. **PowerPoint Slides 3.1–3.14**

4. Videos

   a. **Video 3.1**: "Close reading with sixth-grade English language learners."

   b. **Video 3.2**: "Students rereading and discussing a complex text in high school English."

   c. **Video 3.3**: "Close reading of historical information."

   d. **Video 3.4**: "Close reading and text-dependent questions in upper elementary school."

   e. **Video 3.5**: "Close reading in the primary grades."

   f. **Video 3.6**: "Teacher working with groups of students to facilitate their understanding."

   g. **Video 3.7**: "Teacher using prompts and cues to guide learning."

   h. **Video 3.8**: "Teacher working with small groups of students to generate questions."

▶ Segment I: Approximately 3 Minutes
Stating the Purpose of This Session

   a. Project **PowerPoint Slide 3.1** to begin Segment I.

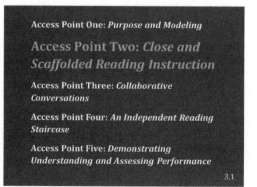

Access Point One: *Purpose and Modeling*

Access Point Two: *Close and Scaffolded Reading Instruction*

Access Point Three: *Collaborative Conversations*

Access Point Four: *An Independent Reading Staircase*

Access Point Five: *Demonstrating Understanding and Assessing Performance*

3.1

b. Project **PowerPoint Slide 3.2:** What's Our Purpose for Module 3? Read through it with participants.

  i. Understand how close and scaffolded reading instruction will support students in their gradual shift in assuming responsibility for their learning through:

   1. Understanding and examining the Six Essential Practices of Close Reading Instruction.

   2. Exploring the Four Principles of Scaffolded Instruction, and understanding how questions, prompts, and cues are integral to the practice of scaffolded instruction.

  ii. Understand how these two instructional practices support Anchor Standards 1 and 10.

What's Our Purpose for Module 3?

Understand how **close** and **scaffolded reading instruction** will support students in their **gradual shift** in assuming **responsibility** for their **learning** through

  ◇ Understanding and examining the **Six Essential Practices** of Close Reading Instruction.

  ◇ Exploring the **Four Principles** of Scaffolded Instruction, and understanding how **questions**, **prompts**, and **cues** are **integral** to the practice of scaffolded instruction.

Understand how these two instructional practices **support Anchor Standards 1** and **10.**

3.2

▶ Segment II: Approximately 10 Minutes
Up Close With Close Reading

a. Provide participants with a brief background of close reading. (Note: depending on your group, you may want the participants to read this section in the text and then share salient points with the whole group). If you wish, project **PowerPoint Slide 3.3.** Share notable points that were not mentioned (also found in **PowerPoint Slide 3.3**'s notes section):

  i. It is not new practice.

  ii. Use with texts that are worthy: it is not for all texts (mentioned in Chapter 1 and in Module 1, Segment III).

  iii. Texts should be complex enough to undergo repeated readings for deep analysis (mentioned in Chapter 1 and in Module 1, Segment III).

iv. Foremost during a close read, the reader is focused on the author's meaning.

v. Close readings should be directed in all content classes in which complex texts play a role because each discipline and/or subject area has texts with distinctive characteristics to analyze and interpret.

vi. Close reading instruction may be used K–12.

vii. There are six guiding practices for all close reading instruction, regardless of the content.

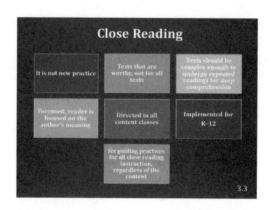

▶ Segment III: Approximately 15 Minutes
Close Reading With English Language Learners

a. Watch **Video 3.1:** "Close reading with sixth-grade English language learners."

b. After the video, have participants turn and talk with a colleague about observations of the lesson.

c. Share relevant points with the whole group.

▶ Segment IV: Approximately 1 Hour 20 Minutes (if you choose to view all videos)
Examining and Observing the Six Practices of Close Reading

Project **PowerPoint Slide 3.4.**

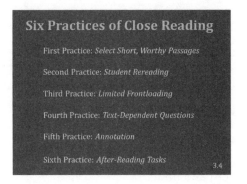

Because there are three videos, each one corresponding with one of the six practices, it is best to examine, as a whole group, each practice individually.

First Practice: Select Short, Worthy Passages (Approximately 10 Minutes)

a. Find the section titled Select Short, Worthy Passages in Chapter 3 of this book, pages 46–47. Have participants read, highlight, and note significant features of the practice (i.e., short, worthy passages and why they are significant) .

b. Have participants share their findings with the whole group.

c. If you wish, project **PowerPoint Slide 3.5.** Here are a few important points to share, if not mentioned:

   i. Normally a passage between three and nine paragraphs in length is best for practicing analytic skills.

   ii. Texts should be deeply understood by the teacher in order to know where the complex and difficult parts may inhibit student understanding.

   iii. Texts do not need to be stand-alone texts.

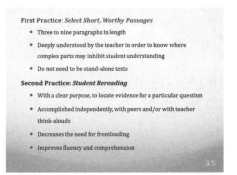

Second Practice: Student Rereading
(Approximately 20 Minutes)

a. In the book, have participants read, highlight, and note significant features of the practice, and why they are significant.

b. Have participants share their findings.

c. Next, have participants view **Video 3.2:** "Students rereading and discussing a complex text in high school English," looking for elements they read about and noticed.

d. Discuss the participants' observations.

e. If you wish, project **PowerPoint 3.5.** Here are a few significant points to share, if not mentioned:

    i. Rereadings should have a clear *purpose*, and are frequently connected to looking for evidence to a particular question. (Clear, quality purpose statements are discussed in Module 2/Chapter 2.)

    ii. Rereadings may be accomplished independently, with peers and/or with teacher think-alouds.

    iii. Rereading decreases the need for frontloading.

    iv. Rereading improves fluency and comprehension.

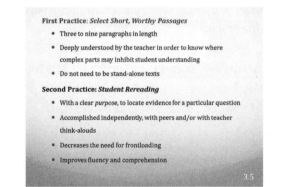

Third Practice: Limited Frontloading
(Approximately 20 Minutes)

a. In the book, have participants read, highlight, and note significant features of the practice, and why they are significant.

b. Have participants share their findings.

c. Next, have participants view **Video 3.3:** "Close reading of historical information," looking for elements they read about and noticed.

d. Discuss their observations.

e. If you wish, project **PowerPoint Slide 3.6.** Here are a few key points to share if not mentioned:

    i. There is very little pre-teaching or frontloading by the teacher.

    ii. The inquiry through rereading that results in the discovery of the author's meaning helps develop metacognitive skills.

    iii. Too much frontloading or pre-teaching limits students' opportunity for inquiry and discovery; these are essential for students to become critical, independent readers.

Third Practice: *Limited Frontloading*

- Limited pre-teaching or frontloading by the teacher
- Inquiry through rereading results in the discovery of the author's meaning and helps develop metacognitive skills
- Too much limits students' opportunities for inquiry and discovery; these are essential for becoming critical, independent readers

Fourth Practice: *Text-Dependent Questions*

- Question types that are asked affect how a reader reads
- Allow students to provide evidence from the text rather than from their own experiences
- Help build foundational knowledge so students are equipped to then formulate meaningful connections and opinions
- Scaffold understanding from explicit to implicit
- Requires preparation by the teacher for thorough text discussion and analysis

3.6

Fourth Practice: Text-Dependent Questions (Approximately 20 Minutes)

a. Have participants read, highlight, and note significant features of the practice, and why they are significant.

b. Have participants share their findings.

c. Next, have participants view **Video 3.4:** "Close reading and text-dependent questions in upper elementary school," looking for elements they read about and noticed.

d. Discuss their observations and insights.

e. If you wish, project **PowerPoint Slide 3.6.** Here are notable points to share if not mentioned:

i. Question types that are asked affect how a reader reads.

ii. Text-dependent questions should allow students to provide evidence from the text rather than their own experiences.

iii. These types of questions help build foundational knowledge, so students are equipped to then formulate meaningful connections and opinions.

iv. If you wish, project **PowerPoint Slide 3.8**: The Six Types of Text-Dependent Questions that scaffold understanding from explicit to implicit.

v. Requires preparation by the teacher for thorough text discussion and analysis.

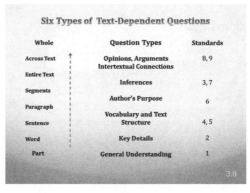

Fifth Practice: Annotation (Approximately 15 Minutes)

a. Have participants read, highlight, and note significant features of the practice annotation and why they are significant.

b. Have participants share their findings.

c. Discuss their observations and insights.

d. If you wish, project **PowerPoint Slide 3.7.** Here are a few noteworthy points to share if not mentioned:

i. When students are allowed to mark up the text, they play an active role in growing their knowledge and understanding.

ii. Annotation should be completed with each rereading guided by text-dependent questions.

iii. Use student annotations as formative assessments.

iv. Annotation slows the readers down for deeper understanding, so it becomes a habit of mind.

v. Use universal annotation marks. Project **PowerPoint Slide 3.9:** Universal Annotation Marks

vi. There is no wrong answer in annotating, the only wrong thing is not to annotate.

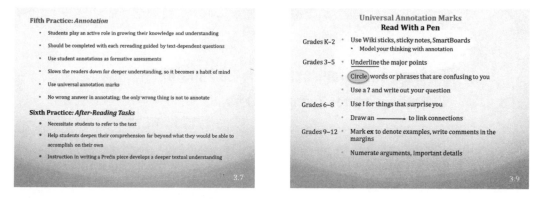

Sixth Practice: After-Reading Tasks (Approximately 10 Minutes)

a. In the book, have participants read, highlight, and note significant features of the practice and why they are significant.

b. Have participants share their findings.

c. Discuss their observations and insights.

d. If you wish, project **PowerPoint Slide 3.7.** Here are a few notable points to share if not mentioned:

i. Post-reading tasks should require students to refer back to the text.

ii. Tasks should help students deepen their comprehension far beyond what they would be able to accomplish on their own.

iii. Instruction in writing a Précis piece develops a deeper textual understanding of the text, as it should be a clear and concise summary of the essential points, without a personal opinion or connection.

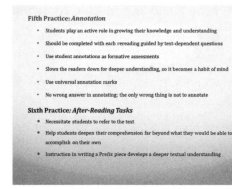

Fifth Practice: *Annotation*

• Students play an active role in growing their knowledge and understanding

• Should be completed with each rereading guided by text-dependent questions

• Use student annotations as formative assessments

• Slows the readers down for deeper understanding, so it becomes a habit of mind

• Use universal annotation marks

• No wrong answer in annotating; the only wrong thing is not to annotate

Sixth Practice: *After-Reading Tasks*

• Necessitate students to refer to the text

• Help students deepen their comprehension far beyond what they would be able to accomplish on their own

• Instruction in writing a Précis piece develops a deeper textual understanding

37

▶ Segment V: Approximately 20 Minutes
Close Reading for Young Readers, K–3

a. Find the section titled Close Reading for Young Readers in Chapter 3 in *Rigorous Reading,* pages 60–63. Have participants read, highlight, and note significant features of the practice and why they are significant.

b. Have participants share their findings.

c. Have participants view **Video 3.5:** "Close reading in the primary grades," looking for elements they read about and noticed.

d. Discuss their observations.

e. If you wish, project **PowerPoint Slide 3.10**. Here are a few notable points to share if not mentioned:

    i. Exposure to complex texts challenges students' thinking.

    ii. Two instructional practices for close reading (close listening):

        1. *Interactive Read-Alouds* (Fisher, Flood, Lapp, & Frey, 2004)— same practices: a short, worthy text, text-dependent questions, limited frontloading, and after-listening tasks to refer back to the text, as grades 3–12, except there is no annotation.

        2. Shared Reading—all the same practices for grades 3–12, but simple annotation and after-listening tasks.

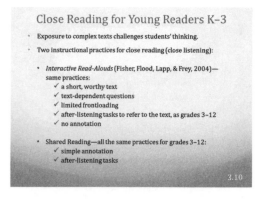

Close Reading for Young Readers K–3

- Exposure to complex texts challenges students' thinking.

- Two instructional practices for close reading (close listening):

  - *Interactive Read-Alouds* (Fisher, Flood, Lapp, & Frey, 2004)—
    same practices:
    - ✓ a short, worthy text
    - ✓ text-dependent questions
    - ✓ limited frontloading
    - ✓ after-listening tasks to refer to the text, as grades 3–12
    - ✓ no annotation

  - Shared Reading—all the same practices for grades 3–12:
    - ✓ simple annotation
    - ✓ after-listening tasks

3.10

▶ Segment VI: Approximately 20 Minutes

Understanding the Four Principles of Scaffold Reading Instruction

a. Project **PowerPoint Slide 3.11:** Directions for Jigsaw Procedure for the Four Principles of Scaffolded Reading Instruction, or provide participants with copies.

b. Have participants form groups to conduct a jigsaw discussion of the Four Principles of Scaffolded Reading Instruction. Use the graphic organizer on page 223 if desired. (You may wish to copy and use this in Modules 4–6 as well).

c. Each person is assigned to read a different short section from *Rigorous Reading* and take notes of the salient points to share with the other group members.

d. View **Video 3.6:** "Teacher working with groups of students to facilitate their understanding."

e. Have participants discuss principles of accessing complex texts that were observed, along with other relevant points.

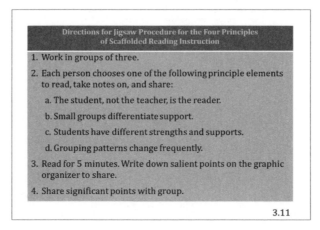

▶ Segment VII: Approximately 30 Minutes
Guiding Readers With Questions and Prompts

a. Questioning is just as essential in scaffolded instruction as it is in close reading instruction; however, the questions used in scaffolded instruction aim to address students' misconceptions and errors while reading.

b. Have participants read and discuss with a partner the section of Chapter 3 titled Questions to Check for Understanding on pages 66–67.

c. Have participants view **Video 3.8:** "Teacher working with small groups of students to generate questions."

d. Discuss significant points from the video.

e. Here are a few notable points to share if not mentioned:

f. Questioning is a time to clear up errors and misunderstandings, not the time for assessment.

g. It is essential to use additional prompts and cues—not provide answers when learners make errors or have misconceptions.

h. Have participants examine and discuss **Figure 3.4:** Types of Prompts.

Figure 3.4 Types of Prompts

Type of Prompt	Definition/When to Use	Examples
Background knowledge	Used when there is content that the student already knows, has been taught, or has experienced but has temporarily forgotten or is using incorrectly.	• As part of a science passage about the water cycle, the teacher asks, "What do you remember about states of matter?" • When reading about a trip to the zoo, the teacher asks, "Remember when we had a field trip to the zoo last month? Do you recall how we felt when it started to rain?"
Process or procedure	Used when established or generally agreed-on rules or guidelines are not being followed and a reminder will help resolve the error or misconception.	• The student is saying a word incorrectly, and the teacher says, "When two vowels go walking. . . ." • When the student has difficulty starting to develop a writing outline, the teacher says, "I'm thinking about the mnemonic we've used for organizing an explanatory article."
Reflective	Used to encourage students to be metacognitive and to think about their thinking, which can then be used to determine next steps or the solution to a problem.	• The student has just read something incorrectly, and the teacher asks, "Does that make sense? Really think about it." • When the student fails to include evidence in her writing, the teacher asks, "What are we learning today? What was our purpose?"
Heuristic	Used to help learners develop their own way to solve problems. These are informal problem-solving procedures. They do not have to be the same as others' heuristics, but they do need to work.	• When the student has difficulty explaining the relationships between characters in a text, the teacher says, "Maybe drawing a visual representation of the main character's connections to one another will help you." • When a student gets stuck and cannot think of what to write next, the teacher says, "Writers have a lot of different ways for getting unstuck. Some just write whatever comes to mind, others create a visual, others talk it out with a reader, and others take a break and walk around for a few minutes. Will any of those help you?"

Source: Adapted from Fisher and Frey (2013a).

▶ Segment VIII: Approximately 20 Minutes
Using Cues to Shift Attention

Cues are warranted when errors and misconceptions have not been cleared with prompts.

a. Have participants read, discuss, and examine with a partner the section of the book titled Cues to Shift Attention on page 70 and **Figure 3.5:** Types of Cues.

Figure 3.5	Types of Cues	
Type of Cue	Definition	Example
Visual	A range of graphic hints that guide students through thinking or understanding.	• Highlighting places on a text where students have made errors • Creating a graphic organizer to arrange content visually • Asking students to take a second look at a graphic or visual from a textbook
Verbal	Variations in speech used to draw attention to something specific or verbal attention getters that focuses students thinking.	• "This is important . . ." • "This is the tricky part. Be careful and be sure to. . . ." • Repeating a student's statement using a questioning intonation • Changing volume or speed of speech for emphasis
Gestural	Teacher's body movements or motions used to draw attention to something that has been missed.	• Pointing to the word wall when a student is searching for the right word or the spelling of a word • Making a hand motion that has been taught in advance such as one used to indicate the importance of summarizing or predicting while reading • Placing thumbs around a key idea in a text that the student was missing
Environmental	Using the surroundings, and things in the surroundings, to influence students' understanding.	• Keeping environmental print current so that students can use it as a reference • Using magnetic letters or other manipulatives to guide student's thinking • Moving an object or person so that the orientation changes and guides thinking

Source: Adapted from Fisher and Frey (2013a).

b. Then have participants view **Video 3.7:** "Teacher using prompts and cues to guide learning." Discuss significant points after the video.

c. It is essential to use prompts and cues, and to not provide answers when learners make errors or have misconceptions.

▶ Segment IX: Approximately 3 Minutes
Summarize the Session With Significant Point

If you wish, project **PowerPoint Slide 3.12** and **Slide 3.13** to help you summarize this session.

a. Round robin reading is ineffective.

b. Choral reading is not appropriate for this type of instruction.

c. Small groups, no more than six, are not static; they should be flexible and change based on ongoing assessments.

d. Instruction is about 10–20 minutes, based on the needs and stamina of students.

e. It is a cognitively demanding time for students.

f. All students benefit from scaffolded instruction, not just your struggling readers.

g. Lessons are tailored to the group's needs, based on recent assessments.

h. Teachers provide more support for students than in a close reading lesson.

i. Questions are essential to scaffolded instruction.

j. A notable point to share if not mentioned:

   i. When cues and prompts are exhausted and misconceptions remain, provide a direct explanation.

Scaffolded Instruction: Be Mindful

- Round robin reading is ineffective.

- Choral reading is not appropriate for this type of instruction.

- Small groups, no more than six, are not static.

- Instruction is 10–20 minutes, based on needs and stamina.

- It is a cognitively demanding time.   3.12

Scaffolded Instruction: Be Mindful

- All students benefit from scaffolded instruction, not just your struggling readers.

- Lessons are tailored to group needs, based on recent assessments.

- Teachers provide more support for students than in a close reading lesson.

- Questions are essential to scaffolded instruction.

- When cues and prompts are exhausted and misconceptions remain, provide a direct explanation.   3.13

▶ WRAP UP: Approximately 3 Minutes
One Final Note

If you wish, project **PowerPoint Slide 3.14.**

a. Close reading and scaffolded reading instruction are vital if we want our students to independently read complex texts.

b. These types of reading instruction allow for the shift in learning responsibility.

c. Scaffolded reading is better for small groups of no more than six, while close reading is effective for whole-group or small-group instruction.

d. Next Access Point: Collaborative Conversations.

One Final Note

- Close reading and scaffolded reading instruction are **vital** if we want our students to **independently read complex texts**.

- These types of reading instruction allow for the **shift** in **learning responsibility**.

- **Scaffolded reading** is better for **small groups** of **no more than six**.

- **Close reading** is effective for **whole-group** or **small-group** instruction.

Next session: Access Point Three: *Collaborative Conversations*

3.14

▶ Supplementary Session: Approximately 30 Minutes

Collaboratively Creating Text-Dependent Questions for Complex Texts

a. In follow-up sessions, such as with grade-level teams, have participants bring a short, worthy passage or an excerpt from a longer passage. If your group has been partaking of the supplementary sessions, have them bring the complex text(s) they have been using for Module 1 and Module 2. If not, have participants bring in a text to use for close reading instruction or supply complex texts for the participants that they could use for their grade level.

b. In collaborative groups, use the **Text-Dependent Questions Template** on page 222 to develop text-dependent questions.

c. Remind participants that they want to create questions that help students discover, through inquiry, the author's meaning and to spark thought-provoking discussions.

d. Refer participants to *Rigorous Reading* Chapter 3 sections on Text-Dependent Questions and Annotation, as well as **Figures 3.2, 3.3, and 3.4** in that chapter. All will provide valuable support for participants in developing these types of evidence-based questions.

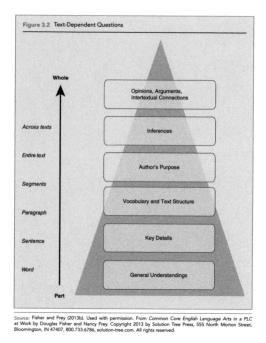

Figure 3.2 Text-Dependent Questions

Whole

| Opinions, Arguments, Intertextual Connections |
| Inferences |
| Author's Purpose |
| Vocabulary and Text Structure |
| Key Details |
| General Understandings |

Across texts

Entire text

Segments

Paragraph

Sentence

Word

Part

Figure 3.3 Sample Text-Dependent Questions

Question Type	Questions From Frog and Toad Together (Lobel, 1971) in First Grade	Questions From Chapter 10 in A Night to Remember (Lord, 1955) in Sixth Grade
General Understandings	Retell the story using *first, next, then,* and *finally.*	Why would the author title the chapter "Go Away"?
Key Details	What ways did they try to solve the problem of eating too many cookies?	What are two things that could have prevented this tragedy?
Vocabulary and Text Structure	How did the author help us to understand what *willpower* means?	How does the chronological structure help the reader understand the events?
Author's Purpose	Who tells the story?	Whose story is most represented and whose story is underrepresented?
Inferences	Do you think Toad's actions caused the seeds to grow? Why?	Why would Mrs. Brown run lifeboat number 6 with a revolver?
Opinions, Arguments, Intertextual Connections	In your opinion, is Frog a good friend to Toad? Do you think this is a happy story or a sad one?	Compare this book with *Inside the Titanic* (Brewster & Marschall, 1997). What are the similarities and differences?

Source: Fisher and Frey (2012a).

Teaching and Reflecting

a. Have participants teach a close reading lesson using the template as a guide.

b. Encourage participants to take notes on the lesson and on student responses.

c. Set another time to reflect and discuss how the close reading instruction went. Use the discussion as a guide for ongoing and future study.

This process may be used in future sessions on developing a Scaffolded Reading Lesson.

Access Point Three

Collaborative Conversations

▶ **Estimated Time: 2 Hours 20 Minutes**

The purpose of Module 4 is for participants to understand the value and necessity of student peer interaction in collaborative learning settings to enable students to independently read complex texts. Participants will do this by analyzing the K–12 Speaking and Listening Anchor Standard 1 from the Common Core State Standards (CCSS). Participants will also closely examine and discuss the essential indicators and key elements of collaborative learning structures. In addition, participants will explore collaborative learning structures: literature circles, discussion roundtables, reciprocal teaching, and collaborative strategic reading.

Materials You Will Need

1. Copies of **Figure 4.1:** Speaking and Listening Anchor Standard 1 (if participants do not have the book)

2. Chart paper and markers for group collaboration and presentations

3. **PowerPoint Slides 4.1–4.9**

4. Videos

    a. **Video 4.1:** "Teacher introduces literature circles."

    b. **Video 4.2:** "Teaching students to collaborate."

    c. **Video 4.3:** "Introducing partner talk."

    d. **Video 4.4:** "Teacher outlining expectations, especially for language usage."

    e. **Video 4.5:** "Students working collaboratively on a presentation."

    f. **Video 4.6:** "Students collaborating to learn content."

    g. **Video 4.7:** "Teacher facilitates a discussion as practice for students' collaborative work."

▶ Segment I: Approximately 3 Minutes
Stating the Purpose of This Session

    a. Project **PowerPoint Slide 4.1** and **Slide 4.2** and state the purpose of this module to the participants:

        i. Understand the value and necessity of student peer interaction in collaborative learning.

        ii. Analyze the differences in grade-level expectations in Speaking and Listening Standard Anchor 1 in CCSS.

        iii. Look closely at the essential indicators and key elements of collaborative learning structures.

        iv. Explore the most effective collaborative learning structures to support students in accessing complex texts: literature circles, discussion roundtables, reciprocal teaching, and collaborative strategic reading.

Access Point One: *Purpose and Modeling*

Access Point Two: *Close and Scaffolded Reading Instruction*

Access Point Three: Collaborative Conversations

Access Point Four: *An Independent Reading Staircase*

Access Point Five: *Demonstrating Understanding and Assessing Performance*

4.1

What's Our Purpose for Module 4?

Understand the **value** and **necessity** of student **peer interaction** in **collaborative learning**.

Analyze the differences in **grade-level expectations** in **Speaking** and **Listening Standard Anchor 1** in CCSS.

Look closely at the **essential indicators** and **key elements** of **collaborative learning structures**.

Explore the most effective **collaborative learning structures** to support students in **accessing complex texts**:
- ❖ literature circles
- ❖ discussion roundtables
- ❖ reciprocal teaching
- ❖ collaborative strategic reading

4.2

▶ Segment II: Approximately 15 Minutes

Understanding the Value of Collaborative Conversations

a. Begin by having participants view **Video 4.2:** "Teaching students to collaborate."

b. After viewing, have participants discuss the merits and characteristics of collaborative conversation as shown in the video and compare with learning in their own classrooms.

c. If you wish, project **PowerPoint Slide 4.3.** Help participants understand, through discussion, that collaboration learning:

   i. Is a critical linchpin in the process of accessing complex texts, as it allows students to work together to improve understanding.

   ii. Supports students learning in the absence of a teacher. Remind participants of the *gradual release of responsibility* (Fisher & Frey, 2008; Pearson & Fielding, 1991) and the Zone of Proximal Development (Vygotsky 1978) model that they discussed in Module 1, Chapter 1.

   iii. Provides opportunities for students to apply skills and strategies modeled during close and scaffolded reading instruction, such as practice in critical thinking, argumentation, and using evidence in their responses.

   iv. Allows for authentic practice of academic language.

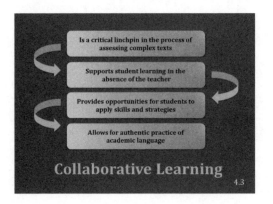

Is a critical linchpin in the process of assessing complex texts

Supports student learning in the absence of the teacher

Provides opportunities for students to apply skills and strategies

Allows for authentic practice of academic language

Collaborative Learning

4.3

▶ Segment III: Approximately 20 Minutes

Analyzing the Speaking and Learning Anchor Standard 1: Prepare for and participate effectively in a range of conversations and collaborations with diverse partners, building on others' ideas and expressing their own, clearly and persuasively.

a. Remind participants that in Module 1 they examined the grade-level progressions for ELA Anchor Standard 1 and 10. Tell participants this time they will analyze the differences between grade-level expectations in the Speaking and Listening Anchor Standard 1.

b. You may want to have participants bring their highlighted ELA Anchor Standards 1 and 10 from Module 1 to compare where the big jumps are between the Reading and Speaking and Listening Standards. It may be helpful to highlight how the standards are interrelated.

c. Group participants in vertical teams, so that each group member is from a different, consecutive grade level.

d. Refer participants to Chapter 4, where they will find **Figure 4.1:** Speaking and Listening Anchor Standard 1.

Figure 4.1	**Speaking and Listening Anchor Standard 1**
SL.CCR.1	CCR Speaking and Listening Anchor Standard 1: Prepare for and participate effectively in a range of conversations and collaborations with diverse partners, building on others' ideas and expressing their own clearly and persuasively.
SL.K.1 Kindergarten Students:	Participate in collaborative conversations with diverse partners about kindergarten topics and texts with peers and adults in small and large groups. a. Follow agreed-upon rules for discussion (e.g., listening to others and taking turns speaking about the topics and texts under discussion.) b. Continue a conversation through multiple exchanges.
SL.1.1 Grade 1 Students:	Engage effectively in a range of collaborative discussions (one-on-one, in groups, and teacher-led) with diverse partners on grade 3 topics and texts, building on others' ideas and expressing their own clearly. a. Come to discussions prepared, having read or studied required material; explicitly draw on that preparation and other information known about the topic to explore ideas under discussion. b. Follow agreed-upon rules for discussions (e.g., gaining the floor in respectful ways, listening to others with care, speaking one at a time about the topics and texts under discussion). c. Ask questions to check understanding of information presented, stay on topic, and link their comments to the remarks of others. d. Explain their own ideas and understanding in light of the discussion.
SL.2.1 Grade 2 Students:	Participate in collaborative conversations with diverse partners about grade 2 topics and texts with peers and adults in small and large groups. a. Follow agreed-upon rules for discussion (e.g., gaining the floor in respectful ways, listening to others with care, speaking one at a time about the topics and texts under discussion.) b. Build on others' talk in conversations by linking their comments to the remarks of others. c. Ask for clarification and further explanation as needed about the topics and texts under discussion.
SL.3.1 Grade 3 Students:	Engage effectively in a range of collaborative discussions (one-on-one, in groups, and teacher-led) with diverse partners on grade 3 topics and texts, building on others' ideas and expressing their own clearly. a. Come to discussions prepared, having read or studied required material; explicitly draw on that preparation and other information known about the topic to explore ideas under discussion. b. Follow agreed-upon rules for discussions (e.g., gaining the floor in respectful ways, listening to others with care, speaking one at a time about the topics and texts under discussion).

(Continued)

	c. Ask questions to check understanding of information presented, stay on topic, and link their comments to the remarks of others. d. Explain their own ideas and understanding in light of the discussion.
SL.4.1 Grade 4 Students:	Engage effectively in a range of collaborative discussions (one-on-one, in groups, and teacher-led) with diverse partners on grade 4 topics and texts, building on others' ideas and expressing their own clearly. a. Come to discussions prepared, having read or studied required material; explicitly draw on that preparation and other information known about the topic to explore ideas under discussion. b. Follow agreed upon rules for discussions and carry out assigned roles. c. Pose and respond to specific questions to clarify or follow upon information, and make comments that contribute to the discussion and link to the remarks of others. d. Review the key ideas expressed and explain their own ideas and understanding in light of the discussion.
SL.5.1 Grade 5 Students:	Engage effectively in a range of collaborative discussions (one-on-one, in groups, and teacher-led) with diverse partners on grade 5 topics and texts, building on others' ideas and expressing their own clearly. a. Come to discussions prepared, having read or studied required material; explicitly draw on that preparation and other information known about the topic to explore ideas under discussion. b. Follow agreed-upon rules for discussions and carry out assigned roles. c. Pose and respond to specific questions by making comments that contribute to the discussion and elaborate on the remarks of others. d. Review the key ideas expressed and draw conclusions in light of information and knowledge gained from the discussions.
SL.6.1 Grade 6 Students:	Engage effectively in a range of collaborative discussions (one-on-one, in groups, and teacher-led) with diverse partners on grade 6 topics, texts, and issues, building on others' ideas and expressing their own clearly. a. Come to discussions prepared, having read or studied required material; explicitly draw on that preparation by referring to evidence on the topic, text, or issue to probe and reflect on ideas under discussion. b. Follow rules for collegial discussions, set specific goals and deadlines, and define individual roles as needed. c. Pose and respond to specific questions with elaboration and detail by making comments that contribute to the topic, text, or issue under discussion. d. Review the key ideas expressed and demonstrate understanding of multiple perspectives through reflection and paraphrasing.

(Continued)

(Continued)

SL.7.1 Grade 7 Students:	Engage effectively in a range of collaborative discussions (one-on-one, in groups, and teacher-led) with diverse partners on grade 7 topics, texts, and issues, building on others' ideas and expressing their own clearly. a. Come to discussions prepared, having read or researched material under study; explicitly draw on that preparation by referring to evidence on the topic, text, or issue to probe and reflect on ideas under discussion. b. Follow rules for collegial discussions, track progress toward specific goals and deadlines, and define individual roles as needed. c. Pose questions that elicit elaboration and respond to others' questions and comments with relevant observations and ideas that bring the discussion back on topic as needed. d. Acknowledge new information expressed by others and, when warranted, modify their own views.
SL.8.1 Grade 8 Students:	Engage effectively in a range of collaborative discussions (one-on-one, in groups, and teacher-led) with diverse partners on grade 8 topics, texts, and issues, building on others' ideas and expressing their own clearly. a. Come to discussions prepared, having read or researched material under study; explicitly draw on that preparation by referring to evidence on the topic, text, or issue to probe and reflect on ideas under discussion. b. Follow rules for collegial discussions and decision-making, track progress toward specific goals and deadlines, and define individual roles as needed. c. Pose questions that connect the ideas of several speakers and respond to others' questions and comments with relevant evidence, observations, and ideas. d. Acknowledge new information expressed by others, and, when warranted, qualify or justify their own views in light of the evidence presented.
SL.9-10.1 Grade 9–10 Students:	Initiate and participate effectively in a range of collaborative discussions (one-on-one, in groups, and teacher-led) with diverse partners on grades 9–10 topics, texts, and issues, building on others' ideas and expressing their own clearly and persuasively. a. Come to discussions prepared, having read and researched material under study: explicitly draw on that preparation by referring to evidence from texts and other research on the topic or issue to stimulate a thoughtful, well-reasoned exchange of ideas. b. Work with peers to set rules for collegial discussions and decision-making (e.g., informal consensus, taking votes on key issues, presentation of alternative views), clear goals and deadlines, and individual roles as needed. c. Propel conversations by posing and responding to questions that relate the current discussion to broader themes or larger ideas; actively incorporate others into the discussion; and clarify, verify, or challenge ideas and conclusions.

	d. Respond thoughtfully to diverse perspectives, summarize points of agreement and disagreement, and, when warranted, qualify or justify their own views and understanding and make new connections in light of the evidence and reasoning presented.
SL.11-12.1 Grade 11–12 Students:	Initiate and participate effectively in a range of collaborative discussions (one-on-one, in groups, and teacher-led) with diverse partners on grades 11–12 topics, texts, and issues, building on others' ideas and expressing their own clearly and persuasively. a. Come to discussions prepared, having read and researched material under study; explicitly draw on that preparation by referring to evidence from text and other research on the topic or issue to stimulate a thoughtful, well-reasoned exchange of ideas. b. Work with peers to promote civil, democratic discussions and decision-making, set clear goals and deadlines, and individual roles as needed. c. Propel conversations by posing and responding to questions that probe reasoning and evidence; ensure a hearing for a full range of positions on a topic or issue; clarify, verify, or challenge ideas and conclusions; and promote divergent and creative perspectives. d. Respond thoughtfully to diverse perspectives; synthesize comments, claims, and evidence made on all sides of an issue; resolve contradictions when possible; and determine what additional information or research is required to deepen the investigation or complete the task.

e. Have them discuss the subtleties of the changes and the main differences between grade levels required for students to reach Speaking and Listening Anchor Standard 1. How might teaching and learning be affected?

f. Have groups reflect on new concepts and skills that are introduced at their grade level. Reflect on the importance of meeting Speaking and Listening Anchor Standard 1. If you wish, project **PowerPoint Slide 4.4.**

▶ Segment IV: Approximately 45 Minutes

Understanding Quality Indicators of Task Complexity to Build Strong Structures for Collaborative Learning

a. View **Video 4.3:** "Introducing partner talk."

b. Discuss the how this structure, partner talk, facilitates access to complex texts.

c. Project **PowerPoint Slide 4.5:** Directions for Jigsaw Procedure for Quality Indicators of Task Complexity to Build Strong Structures for Collaborative Learning, or pass out copies of the instructions.

d. Ask participants to follow the instructions for the jigsaw technique, first by selecting a focus from the below list of the Quality Indicators of Task Complexity for each group:

　i. Designs that require students to work together.

　ii Structures that elevate academic language.

　iii. Structures that ensure grade-level work.

　iv. Design for productive failure.

e. When all groups have completed the activity, ask groups that have Task Complexity Indicator 1 and 2 to present first.

f. When the group(s) with the second indicator, *structures that elevate academic language*, have finished their presentations, view **Video 4.4:** "Teacher outlining expectations, especially for language usage."

g. Discuss as a whole group the key points presented in the video. Also discuss observations regarding the use of academic language in the video.

h. Groups continue to present their indicators.

i. After the last presentation on the final task complexity indicator, *design for productive failure,* view **Video 4.5:** "Students working collaboratively on a presentation."

j. Discuss as a whole group the key points presented. Also discuss any observations they made regarding the indicators of task complexity.

k. Ask participants to discuss current strengths and needs regarding these structures. What needs to happen to build in these strong structures in their classrooms?

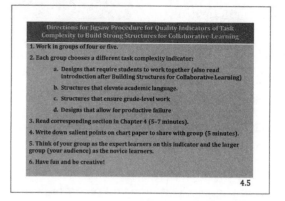

Directions for Jigsaw Procedure for Quality Indicators of Task
Complexity to Build Strong Structures for Collaborative Learning

1. Work in groups of four or five.

2. Each group chooses a different task complexity indicator:

    a. Designs that require students to work together (also read introduction after Building Structures for Collaborative Learning)

    b. Structures that elevate academic language.

    c. Structures that ensure grade-level work

    d. Designs that allow for productive failure

3. Read corresponding section in Chapter 4 (5–7 minutes).

4. Write down salient points on chart paper to share with group (5 minutes).

5. Think of your group as the expert learners on this indicator and the larger group (your audience) as the novice learners.

6. Have fun and be creative!

4.5

▶ Segment V: Approximately 20 Minutes
Recognizing Key Elements of Collaborative Learning

a. Have participants remain in the same groups. This time each participant in the group reads, then shares with their group, significant findings from one of the key elements of collaborative learning:

    i. grouping

    ii. goal setting

    iii. accountability measures of collaborative learning

b. View **Video 4.6:** "Students collaborating to learn content."

c. Have participants reflect, in writing, on elements they feel they implement very well, or that they need to strengthen; this should be a focus for future work. Share with a partner.

d. Summarize the importance of these key elements with **PowerPoint Slides 4.6–4.7:** Quality Indicators and Key Elements of Collaborative Learning.

▶ Segment VI: Approximately 30 Minutes
Exploring Collaborative Learning Structures for Student Engagement in Complex Texts

a. Have participants form new groups, no larger than six per group; encourage participants to work with new people.

b. Each group will examine *one* of the four structures for student engagement in complex texts and will report back to the large group with a presentation:

    i. literature circles

    ii. discussion roundtables

    iii. reciprocal teaching

    iv. collaborative strategic reading

c. Provide chart paper and markers for participants if needed.

d. Have literature circle groups share charts of important points with the whole group first. After the literature circle groups have presented their key points, view **Video 4.1:** "Teacher introduces literature circles." Discuss key points from observations and group presentation.

e. Continue, with all groups presenting. After all groups have presented, view the final **Video 4.7:** "Teacher facilitates a discussion as practice for students' collaborative work."

f. If you wish, project **PowerPoint Slide 4.8.** Have participants think about their current practices/structures for student collaboration. What works well? What can be improved? Are students engaged? What may you need or want more support in? Share with a partner or through a Learning Management System if your school site has one—or start a thread on Edmodo.

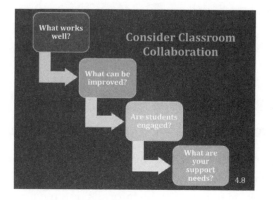

▶ Wrap Up: Approximately 5 Minutes
One Final Note

Project **PowerPoint Slide 4.9.**

a. Remind participants that through their collaborations today they probably reread the text, talked with group members to analyze and synthesize meaning, and used specialized (academic) language for this content. This is similar to what we are asking our students to do!

b. Ask participants to reflect on the following:

   i. Did all your group members contribute to the task?

   ii. Did I contribute to the task?

c. These reflective questions can lead participants to consider issues they may encounter with their students and to think about ways they might revise an activity to deal with such an issue.

d. Inform participants of the access point for the next session: Access Point Four: Independent Reading Staircase

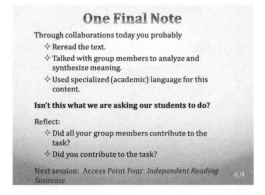

▶ Supplementary Segments: Approximately 30 Minutes

Mini Focus Groups of Collaborative Learning Structures

Participants who are interested in enhancing their knowledge and practical application of the learning structures can form small groups of three to six people to meet. Meetings may be informal, but have a similar structure:

a. Revisit the text for guidance and create a lesson to apply.

b. Teach the lesson in the classroom.

c. Debrief the lesson: what went well, what did not work so well, what were the student responses?

d. Revisit the text/research.

e. Collaborative Planning: modify lessons, or plan new lessons based on what went well and what did not work well.

f. If possible, review video lessons to reflect and plan collaborative meetings in the future.

Access Point Four

An Independent Reading Staircase

▶ **Estimated Time: 2 Hours**

The purpose of Module 5 is for participants to understand the goal of independent learning, which empowers students to develop self-regulations skills, increase their sense of competence, and set their own goals. Participants will also analyze the similarities and differences between independent reading and sustained silent reading (SSR). Additionally, they will examine the four elements of reading conferences, the purpose of reading conferences, and understand how to use conferences for formative assessments.

Materials You Will Need

1. Copies of **Figure 5.1:** Reading Conference Form, **Figure 5.2:** Relationship Between Achievement and Independent Reading, **Figure 5.3:** Differences Between SSR and Independent Reading, and

Figure 5.8: Reading Journal Format for Sequence Stories (if participants do not have *Rigorous Reading* with them).

2. **PowerPoint Slides 5.1–5.10**

3. Copies of **Four Principles of Scaffolded Reading Instruction Graphic Organizer** for notes

4. Videos

    a. **Video 5.1:** "Doug discusses independent learning."

    b. **Video 5.2:** "A student discusses SSR."

    c. **Video 5.3:** "Teachers talk about the use of independent reading."

    d. **Video 5.4:** "Nancy discusses the role of conferencing during reading."

▶ Segment I: Approximately 3 Minutes
Stating the Purpose of this Session

    a. Project **PowerPoint Slide 5.1** and **Slide 5.2** and introduce the purpose of this lesson.

        i. To understand the goal of independent learning when students are accessing complex texts: that they are able to use the literacy strategies that have been taught—during modeling, close reading instruction, scaffolded reading instruction, and collaborative learning structures—and practice building effective reading habits.

        ii. To examine how we can nurture student development through independent reading and sustained silent reading and support this through conferences.

        iii. To analyze the similarities and differences between independent reading and silent sustained reading.

        iv. To examine closely the four elements of conferences, and understand how to use conferences for formative assessments

▶ Segment II: Approximately 15 Minutes

Delving Into the Goals of Independent Learning

a. Communicate to participants the guiding principle of CCSS: When students achieve a competent level of independence, there are increasingly greater possibilities for them to better express their own thoughts and ideas, and to further understand the thoughts and ideas of others.

b. Have participants view **Video 5.1:** "Doug discusses independent learning." After watching the video, have participants turn and talk about the key points or implications.

c. Ask for volunteers to share responses with the whole group.

d. Project **PowerPoint Slide 5.3.** and sum up with the following points:

   i. Independent learning is not a time to have students complete workbook pages or worksheets or assign quiet busy work

   ii. Goal of independent learning is:

      1. To empower students to develop self-regulation skills

      2. For students to increase their sense of competence

      3. For students to set their own goals

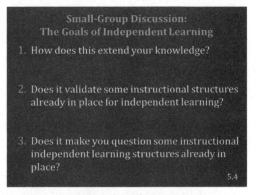

Goals of Independent Learning

1. Independent learning ≠ workbook pages, worksheets, or busy work.

2. Goals of independent learning are
   ➤ To **empower** students to develop **self-regulation skills**
   ➤ For students to **increase** their **sense of competence**
   ➤ For students to **set their own goals**

5.3

e. If they have not done so already, have participants independently read the section titled The Goals of Independent Learning, in Chapter 5, pages 100–101.

f. Afterward, ask participants to form groups of no more than four people and discuss the reading. If you wish, project **PowerPoint Slide 5.4.**

   i. How does this extend your knowledge?

   ii. Does it validate some instructional structures already in place for independent learning?

   iii. Does it make you question some instructional independent learning structures already in place?

> **Small-Group Discussion:**
> **The Goals of Independent Learning**
>
> 1. How does this extend your knowledge?
>
> 2. Does it validate some instructional structures already in place for independent learning?
>
> 3. Does it make you question some instructional independent learning structures already in place?
>
> 5.4

▶ Segment III: Approximately 30 Minutes

Examining Independent Reading so Students can Access Complex Texts

a. Project **PowerPoint Slide 5.5:** Directions for Jigsaw Procedure for Examining Independent Reading to Assess Complex Texts or pass out copies of the instructions.

b. Using the jigsaw technique, have participants get into groups of no more than four. Have each person read a section from *Rigorous Reading* on independent reading:

    i. Vignette (Introduction) at the beginning of Chapter 5 and **Figure 5.1:** Reading Conference Form

Figure 5.1 Reading Conference Form

Student Reading Conference

Name: _____ Date: _____

Title and Author: _____

Retelling (check all that apply)

- ☐ discusses important events
- ☐ offers salient details
- ☐ uses evidence from the text to support retelling
- ☐ states opinion
- ☐ provides textual support for opinion
- ☐ needs prompts to expand answers

Notes:

Oral Reading Fluency

- ☐ reads accurately
- ☐ fluently, in long phrases
- ☐ choppy, in short phrases
- ☐ word by word
- ☐ with expression
- ☐ flat and without expression

Notes:

Goals for Next Meeting

    ii. Introduction after Accessing Complex Texts Requires Independent Reading

    iii. Reading Volume and **Figure 5.2:** Relationship Between Achievement and Independent Reading

Figure 5.2 Relationship Between Achievement and Independent Reading

Percentile Rank	Minutes of Reading per Day (Books)	Words Read per Year
98	65.0	4,358,000
90	21.1	1,823,000
80	14.2	1,146,000
70	9.6	622,000
60	6.5	432,000
50	4.6	282,000
40	3.2	200,000
30	1.8	106,000
20	0.7	21,000
10	0.1	8,000
2	0.0	0

Source: Adapted from Anderson et al. (1988). Used with permission.

    iv. Positive Reading Attitudes

c. Have participants make notes on salient points to share with their group members.

d. View **Video 5.3:** "Teachers talk about the use of independent reading."

e. Have participants share concerns, points of interest, or validating points.

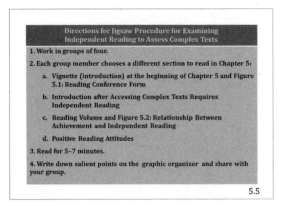

Directions for Jigsaw Procedure for Examining
Independent Reading to Assess Complex Texts

1. Work in groups of four.

2. Each group member chooses a different section to read in Chapter 5:

   a. Vignette (introduction) at the beginning of Chapter 5 and Figure 5.1: Reading Conference Form

   b. Introduction after Accessing Complex Texts Requires Independent Reading

   c. Reading Volume and Figure 5.2: Relationship Between Achievement and Independent Reading

   d. Positive Reading Attitudes

3. Read for 5–7 minutes.

4. Write down salient points on the graphic organizer and share with your group.

5.5

▶ Segment IV: Approximately 30 Minutes
Analyzing the Differences Between Independent Reading and SSR

a. Have participants read **Figure 5.3:** Differences Between SSR and Independent Reading, and each corresponding section in the book. As they read, ask them to think about which autonomous reading structure they employ in their classroom.

Figure 5.3 Differences Between SSR and Independent Reading	Sustained Silent Reading	Independent Reading
Goals and purpose	• Reading for pleasure	• Building mastery through practice
Book selection	• Student choice with a wide range of genres and levels	• Constrained choice of increasingly complex texts
Accountability	• No records kept	• Logs and reflections are essential
What are students doing?	• Reading quietly	• Reading and writing reflections • Conferring with teacher
What is the teacher doing?	• Brief book talk • Reading quietly	• Conferring with students • Observing • Assessing
Follow-up activity	• Students can volunteer to briefly talk about a book; this is not always a part of an SSR session	• Students discuss their reading. The discussion is related to the purpose set at the beginning of the session

b. View **Video 5.2:** "A student discusses SSR."

c. After reading, viewing, and reflecting, have participants begin a whole-group conversation. If you wish, project **PowerPoint Slide 5.6.** Here are a few conversation starters:

   i. When students are reading by themselves, are we providing the most effective support?

   ii. In particular, are we providing support for students to access complex texts when they are reading and practicing strategies that we have been modeling and taught in close reading and scaffolded reading instruction?

   iii. Is there any element in one or both structures that needs refinement?

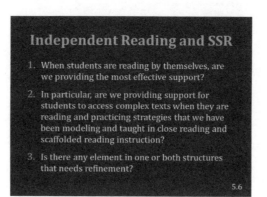

▶ Segment V: Approximately 20 Minutes
Students Responding and Talking During Independent Reading

a. Project **PowerPoint Slide 5.7:** Students Respond During Independent Reading, or provide participants with a copy of the instructions.

b. Using the jigsaw technique, have participants get into groups of no more than four. Encourage participants to change their groups, as we do with our students, to interact with different participants for different perspectives.

c. Have each person in a group read a different section of Chapter 5 under the heading Students Respond During Independent Reading. The sections are

i. Introduction and Sticky Notes

ii. Reading Logs

iii. Reflection Journals

iv. Students Talk About Texts and **Figure 5.8**

Figure 5.8   Reading Journal Format for Sequence Stories

Title of book: _____   Author: _____

This book was about

The best part of this book was

One way the author could change this book is

Here's what happened in the text (use pictures and words)

1	2	3
4	5	6

d. Have each participant make notes on salient points to share with their group members.

e. Have participants discuss which task(s) they currently use, if any, and which they would like to try, or refine.

f. Have participants share concerns, points of interest, or validating points.

g. Project **PowerPoint Slide 5.8.** Sum up this section with the following key points:

   i. Book conversations provide occasions to sharpen listening skills (mentioned in Module 4/Chapter 4).

   ii. Students become mindful of their learning through these tasks and interactions, which in turn builds their metacognitive skills.

   iii. If students are to be sharing in collaborative conversations, they should be explicitly taught *how*.

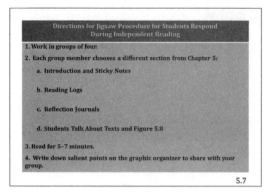

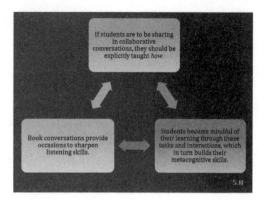

▶ Segment VI: Approximately 20 Minutes

Conferring With Students

a. Have participants view **Video 5.4:** "Nancy discusses the role of conferencing during reading."

b. After the video, have participants turn and talk with a partner about the significant points and issues that Nancy discusses.

c. Project **PowerPoint Slide 5.9:** Four Elements of Effective Conferences. Discuss the purpose of conferring with students as well as the four elements of an effective conference.

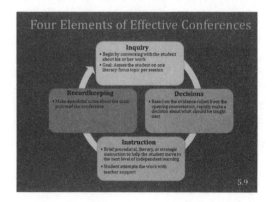

▶ Wrap Up: Approximately 3 Minutes
One Final Note

a. Project **PowerPoint Slide 5.10** and sum up this module for participants:

    i. For students to develop essential reading and thinking habits, which are vital for successful college and career lives, they need to consistently read independently, and confer with teachers about their reading.

b. Inform participants of the topic for the next session: Access Point Five: Demonstrating Understanding and Assessing Performance

One Final Note

For students to develop essential reading and thinking habits, which are vital for successful college and career lives, they need to consistently read independently and confer with teachers about their reading.

Next session: Access Point Five: *Demonstrating Understanding and Assessing Performance*

5.10

▶ Supplementary Segments: Approximately 30 Minutes
Mini Focus Study Group

Participants who are interested in enhancing their knowledge and practical application on the Students Responding and Talking During Independent Reading or Conferring, can form small groups of three to six people. Meetings may be informal but have a similar structure:

a. Revisit the text for guidance and create lessons to apply

b. Teach the lesson in the classroom

c. Debrief the lesson: what went well, what did not work so well, what were the student responses?

d. Revisit the text/research

e. Collaborative Planning: modify lessons, or plan new lessons based on what went well and what did not work well.

To improve the practice of student-teacher reading conferences, ask participants to video themselves conferring with a student. Have them bring their short video to share with the other group members to discuss and address issues that the participant would like to address in conferring.

Access Point Five

Demonstrating Understanding and Assessing Performance

▶ **Estimated Time: 3 Hours**

The purpose of Module 6 is to help participants understand how to assign effective text-dependent tasks that engage students with complex texts; this will develop their metacognitive skills and better prepare them for the demands of college and their careers. Additionally, participants will examine formative assessments, such as feedback, to understand the influence that varying types of feedback have on developing and cultivating students' ability to analyze complex texts. Participants will also become familiar with types of effective feedback for the individual and the class as a whole, and what it means to "feed-up" with error analysis.

Materials You Will Need

1. **PowerPoint Slides 6.1–6.11**

2. Copies of **Figure 6.2**: Feedback Examples and **Figure 6.3**: Grade 2 Error Analysis of Anchor Standard 5 Related to Informational Text (if participants do not have *Rigorous Reading* with them)

3. Copies of **Four Principles of Scaffolded Reading Instruction Graphic Organizer** for notes

4. Videos

   a. **Video 6.1:** "Teacher reflects on her close reading instruction."

   b. **Video 6.2:** "Teacher promotes students' reflection and metacognition after lesson."

   c. **Video 6.3:** "Sample student debate."

   d. **Video 6.4:** "Daily checks for understanding help teachers identify instructional needs."

   e. **Video 6.5:** "A teacher discusses his use of error analysis."

   f. **Video 6.6:** "Teacher reteaches students to use evidence after the error analysis revealed a need."

   g. **Video 6.7:** "Nancy leads a group of teachers in a data review."

▶ Segment I: Approximately 3 Minutes
Stating the Purpose of This Session

a. Project **PowerPoint Slides 6.1** and **6.2** and introduce the purpose of Module 6:

b. To understand how to assign effective text-dependent tasks so that student engagement with complex texts will develop their metacognitive skills and better prepare them for the demands of college and their future careers.

   i. Examine the influence of feedback on students accessing complex texts.

   ii. Consider the value of formative assessments in cultivating our students' ability to access complex texts.

Access Point One: *Purpose and Modeling*

Access Point Two: *Close and Scaffolded Reading Instruction*

Access Point Three: *Collaborative Conversations*

Access Point Four: *An Independent Reading Staircase*

Access Point Five: *Demonstrating Understanding and Assessing Performance*

6.1

What's Our Purpose for Module 6 ?

How to assign **effective text-dependent tasks** so that student **engagement** with complex texts will
◇ Develop **metacognitive** skills
◇ **Prepare** them for the demands of **college** and their future **careers**

Examine the **influence of feedback** on students accessing complex texts.

Consider the value of **formative assessments** in cultivating our **students' ability** to access **complex texts**.

6.2

▶ Segment II: Approximately 20 Minutes

Using Textual Evidence, Not Just Personal Connections, to Access Complex Texts

a. Convey to participants that CCSS standards require students to use textual evidence, compare texts, and analyze the author's meaning.

b. Have participants read the introduction and the dialogue at the beginning of Chapter 6, and then discuss the need to return to the text when reading complex texts.

c. Project **PowerPoint Slide 6.3:** Directions for Jigsaw Procedure for Accessing Complex Texts Requires More Than Personal Connections, or provide participants with a copy of the instructions.

d. Using the jigsaw technique, have participants form groups of no more than four. Have each person in the group read a different section on Accessing Complex Texts Requires More Than Personal Connections:

   i. Model before you expect.

   ii. Pose questions that require students to return to the text.

   iii. Ask students to provide evidence to support their opinions and ideas.

   iv. Require students to write rhetorically.

e. It may be useful to remind participants that points one and two were discussed in greater depth within Modules/Chapters 2 and 3

f. Have participants make notes on salient points to share with their group members.

g. View **Video 6.1:** "Teacher reflects on her close reading instruction."

h. Have participants share concerns, points of interest, and/or validating points.

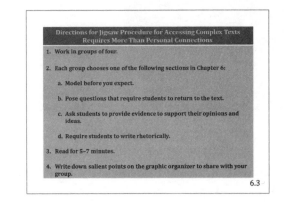

▶ Segment III: Approximately 15 Minutes
Reflecting on the Right After-Reading Task

a. Have participants read the beginning of the section titled Accessing Complex Texts Requires Students to Do Something After Reading, pages 126–127, as it sets the stage for the upcoming video, as well as for reflection of the participants' personal, or schoolwide instructional practices.

b. View **Video 6.2:** "Teacher promotes students' reflection and metacognition after lesson."

c. Have participants share significant points and issues.

▶ Segment IV: Approximately 45 Minutes
Examining Right After-Reading Text-Dependent Tasks

a. Project **PowerPoint Slide 6.4:** Directions for Jigsaw Activity for Text-Dependent Tasks, or provide participants with copies of instructions.

b. Engage the participants in a jigsaw technique of the types of text-dependent tasks.

c. Have participants divide into groups of four to six in a home group. Each member takes a different section from the text-dependent tasks to become an "expert":

    i. perspective writing

    ii. writing to prompts

    iii. Socratic Seminar

    iv. debates

d. Expert groups form by task and spend about five minutes with the book reading about the task.

e. Expert groups take five to seven minutes to discuss main points (implications for accessing complex texts) and to prepare a presentation. Have participants meet back in their home groups to teach the content of the text-dependent task to each other.

f. View **Video 6.3:** "Sample student debate."

g. Discuss with participants how this text-dependent task reinforces returning to text, analytical reasoning, argumentation, refuting, and note taking and how this should be taught and revisited on more than one occasion.

h. Summarize this section with **PowerPoint Slide 6.5:** Types of Text-Dependent Tasks.

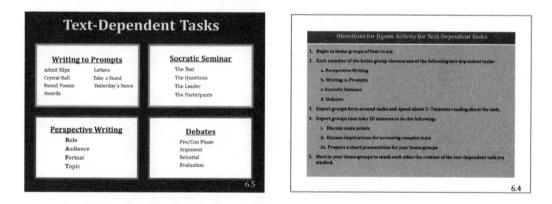

▶ Segment V: Approximately 10 Minutes
Understanding the Need for Formative Assessments

a. Have participants list the ways they currently provide and use formative assessments in their classrooms.

b. In Chapter 6, have participants read the introduction to the section titled Accessing Complex Texts Requires Formative Assessments, page 134.

c. Have them turn and talk with a neighbor about the processes each of them has in place for effective feedback for individual students, and for the whole class.

▶ Segment VI: Approximately 20 Minutes
Looking Closely at the Types of Effective Feedback

a. If you wish, project **PowerPoint Slide 6.6.** Ask participants to look at **Figure 6.2** in the text. Spend some time discussing Hattie and Timperley's (2007) types of feedback and what each means.

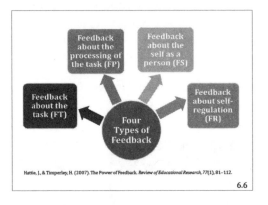

Hattie, J., & Timperley, H. (2007). The Power of Feedback. *Review of Educational Research, 77*(1), 81–112.

6.6

Figure 6.2	Feedback Examples	
Type	Example	Usefulness
Feedback about the task (FT)	"Make sure to change this from a period to an exclamation mark."	Limited
Feedback about the processing of the task (FP)	"You seem to want to emphasize this point. Be sure to use a strong verb to capture that intensity so your reader understands this as well."	Very useful
Feedback about self-regulation (FR)	"Read that passage aloud after you rewrite it to yourself to see if it matches the level of intensity you intend."	Very useful
Feedback about the self as a person (Fs)	"Good boy."	Not useful

b. Project **PowerPoint Slide 6.7.** Ask the group to consider:

i. What type(s) of feedback do you provide most?

ii. Why do you think feedback about the process and self-regulation are the most useful to students?

iii. Why do you think feedback about the student as a person is limiting?

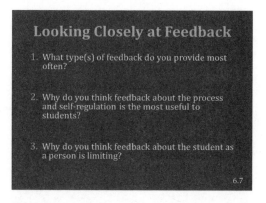

c. Have participants read the section titled Knowing the Individual: Effective Feedback, pages 134–137.

d. Have participants reflect on the ways they provide student feedback and their own strengths and needs in this area. Discuss: what is the outcome when learners are given, or not given, effective feedback?

e. Sum up this session with **PowerPoint Slide 6.8.** If not mentioned in discussion, communicate the following:

i. When effective feedback is not given, the learner is unable to clarify errors and misconceptions. If effective feedback *is* provided, the student is able to move forward in accessing complex texts.

▶ Segment VII: Approximately 15 Minutes
Getting Familiar With Feed-Up

a. Project **PowerPoint Slide 6.9.** Convey to participants that while feedback is primarily intended for the individual, *feed-up* is a process of making instructional decisions based on patterns and trends of the whole class.

> Important Reminders:
>
> ❖ **Feedback** is primarily intended for the **individual**.
>
> ❖ *Feed-up* is a **process** of making **instructional decisions** based on **patterns** and **trends** across groups.
>
> 6.9

b. View **Video 6.4:** "Daily checks for understanding help teachers identify instructional needs."

c. Discuss significant points and issues.

▶ Segment VIII: Approximately 50 Minutes
Understanding the Why and the How of Error Analysis

a. Have participants read the beginning of Knowing the Flock: Feeding Forward, pages 137–140. and **Figure 6.3.**

Skill	Initials of Students Who Are Having Difficulty With This Skill
Locates caption	
Reads caption and relates it to the text	
Reads caption and relates it to the visual information	
Locates bold word	
Describes the role of bold words	
Finds meaning of bold word using glossary	
Locates subheading	
Describes content expected in the section based on the subheading	
Identifies appropriate visual/graphic and caption related to the text in a subheading	

b. View **Video 6.5:** "A teacher discusses his use of error analysis."

c. Discuss the merits and challenges in using error analysis for feedback.

d. Have participants read the section after **Figure 6.3;** then Project **PowerPoint Slide 6.10.** Discuss the purpose of the error analysis:

    i. To identify students who need additional instruction

    ii. To allow teachers to make instructional decisions about what to teach next, or what to *feed-up*.

    iii. To help identify the classes' patterns and trends in learning.

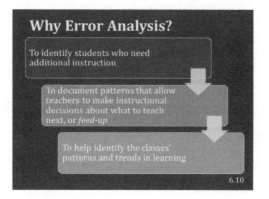

e. View **Video 6.6:** "Teacher reteaches students to use evidence after the error analysis revealed a need."

f. Discuss key points.

g. View **Video 6.7:** "Nancy leads a group of teachers in a data review."

h. Turn and talk with a colleague about the ways in which you now have greater understanding of feedback and how to interpret data for better informed feedback and instruction.

i. Encourage participants to share with the whole group.

▶ Wrap Up: Approximately 3 Minutes
One Final Note

a. Project **PowerPoint Slide 6.11:** One Final Note.

b. Read the quote (one of the authors' favorites) to the participants "You can't fatten a sheep by weighing it." (Brick, 1904).

c. Note that culminating tasks and assessments are never final, because we are constantly observing and assessing our students and planning accordingly for lessons. It's the cycle of effective instruction.

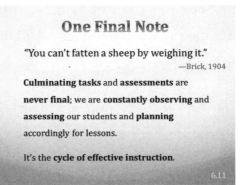

▶ Supplementary Sessions: Approximately 30 Minutes
Mini Focus Study Group

a. Participants who are interested in enhancing their knowledge and practical application in the four Types of Text-Dependent

Tasks—Perspective Writing, Writing to Prompts, Socratic Seminar, and Debates—can form small groups of three to six people to meet. Meetings may be informal but have a similar structure:

i. Revisit the text for guidance and create a lesson to apply

ii. Teach the lesson in the classroom

iii. Debrief the lesson: what went well, what did not work so well, what were the student responses?

iv. Revisit the text/research

v. Collaborative Planning: modify lessons, or plan new lessons based on what went well and what did not work well.

b. Participants may want to work together as a grade level to create Error Analysis Sheets. They can then use them when teaching, meet with their grade levels to discuss the patterns and trends across their grade, or class, and collaborate on next steps of instruction based on the results of the analysis.

Text-Dependent Questions Template		
Question Type		
General Understandings		
Key Details		
Vocabulary and Text Structure		
Author's Purpose		
Inferences		
Opinions, Arguments, Intertextual Connections		

Source: Fisher and Frey (2012a).

Four Principles of Scaffolded Reading Instruction Graphic Organizer

Salient points on the topic or concept:

Section: _____

Section: _____

Section: _____

Section: _____

References

Adler, M. J., & Van Doren, C. (1972). *How to read a book.* New York: Touchstone.

Afflerbach, P., Pearson, P. D., & Paris, S. G. (2008). Clarifying differences between reading skills and reading strategies. *The Reading Teacher, 61*(5), 364–373.

Alexander, P. A., & Jetton, T. L. (2000). Learning from text: A multidimensional and developmental perspective. In M. L. Kamil, P. B. Mosenthal, P. D. Pearson, & R. Barr (Eds.), *Handbook of reading research* (Vol. 3, pp. 285–310). Mahwah, NJ: Erlbaum.

Allington, R. L. (2002). You can't learn much from books you can't read. *Educational Leadership, 60*(3), 16–19.

Anderson, L., Brubaker, N., Alleman-Brooks, J., & Duffy, G. (1985). A qualitative study of seatwork in first-grade classrooms. *Elementary School Journal, 86,* 123–140.

Anderson, R. C., Wilson, P. T., & Fielding, L. G. (1988). Growth in reading and how children spend their time outside school. *Reading Research Quarterly, 23,* 285–303.

Banks, J. A., & Banks, C. A. M. (2012). *Multicultural education: Issues and perspectives* (8th ed.). New York: Wiley.

Baum, L. F. (1900/2000). *The wonderful wizard of Oz.* New York: HarperCollins.

Bennett, N., & Cass, A. (1989). The effects of group composition on group interactive processes and pupil understanding. *British Educational Research Journal, 15*(1), 19–32.

Bonsignore, J. (2001). *Stick out your tongue! Fantastic facts, features, and functions of animal and human tongues.* Atlanta, GA: Peachtree.

Brick, H. (1908). Early spring lambs. *The Farm Journal, 32*(4), 153–154.

Bromley, K. D. (1985). Précis writing and outlining to enhance content learning. *The Reading Teacher, 38*(4), 406–411.

Brown, A. L., & Day, J. D. (1983). Macrorules for summarizing texts: The development of expertise. *Journal of Verbal Learning and Verbal Behavior, 22,* 1–14.

Buehl, D. (2009). *Classroom strategies for interactive learning* (3rd ed.). Newark, DE: International Reading Association.

Campbell, J. R., Voelkl, K. E., & Donahue, P. L. (1997). *NAEP 1996 trends in academic progress* (Report No. NCES-97-986). Princeton, NJ: National Assessment of Educational Progress. (ERIC Document Reproduction Service No. ED411327)

Carle, E. (1996). *The grouchy ladybug.* New York: HarperCollins.

Carroll, C. (1997). *How artists see families.* New York: Abbeville Kids.

Cisneros, S. (1991). *Woman hollering creek, and other stories.* New York: Random House.

Clay, M. M. (2001). *Change over time in children's literacy development.* Portsmouth, NH: Heinemann.

Clements, A. (1996). *Frindle.* New York: Aladdin.

Coleman, D., & Pimentel, S. (2012). Revised publishers' criteria for the Common Core State Standards in English Language Arts and Literacy, grades 3–12. Retrieved from www. corestandards.org/as_sets/Publishers_Criteria_for_3–12.pdf

Council of Chief State School Officers (CCSSO). (2010). *Common core state standards for English language arts and literacy in history/social science, science, and technical subjects.* Retrieved from www.corestandards.org/ELA-Literacy

Daniels, H. (2002). *Literature circles: Voice and choice in book clubs and reading groups* (2nd ed.). York, ME: Stenhouse.

Davey, B. (1983). Think aloud: Modeling the cognitive processes for reading comprehension. *Journal of Reading, 27,* 44–47.

Dean, C. B., Stone, B. J., Hubbell, E., & Pitler, H. (2012). *Classroom instruction that works: Research-based strategies for increasing student achievement* (2nd ed.). Alexandria, VA: ASCD.

Donovan, M. S., & Bransford, J. D. (Eds.). (2005). *How students learn: Science in the classroom.* Washington, DC: National Academies Press.

Elbaum, B., Schumm, J. S., & Vaughn, S. (1997). Urban middle-elementary students' perceptions of grouping formats for reading instruction. *Elementary School Journal, 97,* 475–500.

Fang, Z. (2012). Approaches to developing content area literacies: A synthesis and critique. *Journal of Adolescent & Adult Literacy, 56*(2), 103–108.

Faust, M. A., & Glenzer, N. (2000). "I could read those parts over and over": Eighth graders rereading to enhance enjoyment and learning with literature. *Journal of Adolescent & Adult Literacy, 44,* 234–239.

Fisher, D., Flood, J., Lapp, D., & Frey, N. (2004). Interactive read alouds: Is there a common set of implementation practices? *The Reading Teacher, 58,* 8–17.

Fisher, D., & Frey, N. (2008). *Better learning for structured teaching: A framework for the gradual release of responsibility.* Alexandria, VA: ASCD.

Fisher, D., & Frey, N. (2010a). *Enhancing RTI: How to ensure success with effective classroom instruction and intervention.* Alexandria, VA: ASCD.

Fisher, D., & Frey, N. (2010b). *Guided instruction: How to develop confident and successful learners.* Alexandria, VA: ASCD.

Fisher, D., & Frey, N. (2012a). Close reading in elementary schools. *The Reading Teacher, 66,* 179–188.

Fisher, D., & Frey, N. (2012b). *Improving adolescent literacy: Content area strategies at work* (3rd ed.). Boston: Allyn & Bacon.

Fisher, D., & Frey, N. (2013a). *Better learning through structured teaching: A framework for the gradual release of responsibility* (2nd ed.). Alexandria, VA: ASCD.

Fisher, D., & Frey, N. (2013b). *Common Core English language arts in a PLC at work: Grades 3–5.* Bloomington, IN: Solution Tree.

Fisher, D., Frey, N., Farnan, N., Fearn, L., & Petersen, F. (2004). Increasing writing achievement in an urban middle school. *Middle School Journal, 36*(2), 21–26.

Fisher, D., Frey, N., & Lapp, D. (2008). *In a reading state of mind: Brain research, teacher modeling, and comprehension instruction.* Newark, DE: International Reading Association.

Fisher, D., Frey, N., & Rothenberg, C. (2008). *Content area conversations: How to plan discussion-based lessons for diverse language learners.* Alexandria, VA: ASCD.

Fisher, D., Lapp, D., & Frey, N. (2011). Comprehension: The cooperation of many forces. In D. Lapp & D. Fisher (Eds.), *Handbook of research on teaching the English language arts* (3rd ed.) (pp. 258–263). New York: Routledge.

Fisher, D., Ross, D., & Grant, M. (2010). Building background knowledge in physical science. *The Science Teacher, 77*(1), 23–26.

Fleischman, P. (2006). *Dateline: Troy.* Somerville, MA: Candlewick.

Fountas, I., & Pinnell, G. (2012). Guided reading: The romance and the reality. *The Reading Teacher, 66*(4), 268–284.

Frey, N., & Fisher, D. (2010). Identifying instructional moves during guided learning. *The Reading Teacher, 64*(2), 84–95.

Frey, N., & Fisher, D. (2011). *The formative assessment action plan: Practical steps to more successful teaching and learning.* Alexandria, VA: ASCD.

Frey, N., Fisher, D., & Everlove, S. (2009). *Productive group work: How to engage students, build teamwork, and promote understanding.* Alexandria, VA: ASCD.

Gibson, F. (1956). *Old yeller.* New York: HarperCollins.

Good, T. L., & Brophy, J. E. (2003). *Looking in classrooms* (9th ed.). Boston: Allyn & Bacon.

Graff, G., & Birkenstein, C. (2006). *They say / I say: The moves that matter in academic writing.* New York: W. W. Norton & Company.

Gregory, K. (2001). *Seeds of hope: The gold rush diary of Susanna Fairchild (Dear America).* New York: Scholastic.

Guthrie, J. T., Schafer, W. D., & Huang, C. (2001). Benefits of opportunity to read and balanced instruction on the NAEP. *Journal of Educational Research, 94*, 145–162.

Guthrie, J. T., & Wigfield, A. (2000). Engagement and motivation in reading. In M. L. Kamil, P. B. Mosenthal, P. D. Pearson, & R. Barr (Eds.), *Handbook of reading research* (Vol. 3, pp. 403–424). Mahwah, NJ: Erlbaum.

Hattie, J., & Timperley, H. (2007). The power of feedback. *Review of Educational Research, 77*, 81–112.

Hesse, K. (1996). *The music of dolphins.* New York: Scholastic.

Hiebert, E. H. (Ed.). (2009). *Reading more, reading better: Solving problems in the teaching of literacy.* New York: Guilford.

Holdaway, D. (1979). *The foundations of literacy.* Portsmouth, NH: Heinemann.

Hunter, M. C. (1976). *Improved instruction.* Thousand Oaks, CA: Corwin.

Iowa State University. (2007, May 31). Psychologist explains teens' risky decision-making behavior. *ScienceDaily.* Retrieved from http://www.sciencedaily.com / releases/2007/05/070531093830.htm

Johnson, D., Johnson, R., Holubec, E. J., & Roy, P. (1984). *Circles of learning: Cooperation in the classroom.* Alexandria, VA: ASCD.

Kafka, F. (1946). *Metamorphosis.* New York: Vanguard Press.

Kapur, M. (2008). Productive failure. *Cognition and Instruction, 26*(3), 379–424.

Klinger, J. K., & Vaughn, S. (1998). Using collaborative strategic reading. *TEACHING Exceptional Children, 30*(6), 32–37.

Klinger, J. K., Vaughn, S., & Schumm, J. S. (1998). Collaborative strategic reading during social studies in heterogeneous fourth-grade classrooms. *Elementary School Journal, 99*, 3–20.

Kush, J. C., & Watkins, M. W. (1996). Long-term stability of children's attitudes toward reading. *Journal of Educational Research, 89,* 315–319.

Lobel, A. (1971). *Frog and toad together.* New York: HarperCollins.

Lord, W. (1955). *A night to remember.* New York: St. Martin's Griffin.

Lowry, L. (1989). *Number the stars.* New York: Laurel Leaf.

Marzano, R. J. (2009). *Designing & teaching learning goals and objectives.* Bloomington, IN: Solution Tree.

McLaughlin, M., & DeVoogd, G. L. (2004). *Critical literacy: Enhancing students' comprehension of text.* New York: Scholastic.

Millis, K. K., & King, A. (2001). Rereading strategically: The influences of comprehension ability and a prior reading on the memory for expository text. *Reading Psychology, 22*, 41–65.

National Governors Association Center for Best Practices, Council of Chief State School Officers. (2010). *Common Core State Standards for English language arts and literacy in history/social studies, science, and technical subjects.* Washington, DC: Author. Retrieved from http://www.corestandards.org/the-standards

Newkirk, T. (2010). The case for slow reading. *Educational Leadership, 67*(6), 6–11.

Optiz, M. F., & Rasinski, T. V. (2008). *Good-bye round robin: 25 effective oral reading strategies* (updated ed.). Portsmouth, NH: Heinemann.

Palincsar, A. S., & Brown, A. L. (1984). Reciprocal teaching of comprehension-fostering and comprehension-monitoring activities. *Cognition and Instruction, 1*(2), 117–175.

Pearson, P. D., & Fielding, L. (1991). Comprehension instruction. In R. Barr, M. L. Kamil, P. Mosenthal, & P. D. Pearson (Eds.), *Handbook of reading research* (Vol. 2, pp. 815–860). Mahwah, NJ: Erlbaum.

Pearson, P. D., & Gallagher, M. C. (1983). The instruction of reading comprehension. *Contemporary Educational Psychology, 8,* 317–344.

Pinkney, J. (2009). *The lion and the mouse.* New York: Little, Brown.

Pinnell, G. S., & Fountas, I. C. (2003). Teaching comprehension. *The California Reader, 36*(4), 7–14.

Pressley, M., El-Dinary, P. B., Gaskins, I., Schuder, T., Bergman, J. L., Almasi, J., et al. (1992). Beyond direct explanation: transactional instruction of reading comprehension strategies. *The Elementary School Journal, 92,* 513–555.

Richards, I. A. (1929). *Practical criticism.* London: Cambridge University Press.

Rog, L. J. (2001). *Early literacy instruction in kindergarten.* Newark, DE: International Reading Association.

Rosenblatt, L. M. (1938/1995). *Literature as exploration* (5th ed.). New York: Modern Language Association.

Rosenblatt, L. M. (2003). Literary theory. In J. Flood, D. Lapp, J. R. Squire, & J. M. Jensen (Eds.), *Handbook of research on teaching the English language arts* (pp. 67–73). New York: Macmillan.

Ryan, P. M. (1999). *Riding freedom.* New York: Scholastic.

Santa, C., & Havens, L. (1995). *Creating independence through student-owned strategies: Project CRISS.* Dubuque, IA: Kendall Hunt.

Schunk, D. H. (1998). Goal and self-evaluative influences during children's cognitive skill learning. *American Educational Research Journal, 33,* 359–382.

Sendak, M. (1963). *Where the wild things are.* New York: Harper & Rowe.

Smith, M. C. (1950, June 1). *Declaration of conscience.* US Congress, Senate, Congressional Record, 81st Congress, 2d sess., 7894–7895. Retrieved from http://www.americanrhetoric.com/speeches/margaretchasesmithconscience.html

Smith, M. C. (2000). The real-world reading practices of adults. *Journal of Literacy Research, 32,* 25–52.

Stanovich, K. E. (1986). Matthew effects in reading: Some consequences of individual differences in the acquisition of literacy. *Reading Research Quarterly, 21,* 360–407.

Steinbeck, J. (1945). *The pearl.* New York: Penguin Books.

Stright, A. D., & Supplee, L. H. (2002). Children's self-regulatory behaviors during teacher-directed, seat-work, and small-group instructional contexts, *Journal of Educational Research, 95,* 235–246.

Tatham, B. (2002). *How animals shed their skin.* New York: Franklin Watts.

Tayback, S. (1999). *Joseph had a little overcoat.* New York: Viking.

Tayback, S. (2007). *There was an old lady who swallowed a fly.* Auburn, ME: Child's Play International.

Trivizas, E. (1993). *The three little wolves and the big bad pig.* New York: Aladdin.

Vygotsky, L. S. (1978). *Mind in society: The development of higher psychological processes* (M. Cole, V. John-Steiner, S. Scribner, & E. Souberman, Eds. & Trans.). Cambridge, MA: Harvard University Press.

Weber, K. (Ed.). (2012). *Last call at the oasis: The global water crisis and where we go from here.* New York: PublicAffairs.

Wiesel, E. (1982). *Night.* New York: Bantam.

Wiggins, G. (1998). *Educative assessment: Designing assessments to inform and improve student performance.* San Francisco: Jossey-Bass.

Wiggins, G., & McTighe, J. (2005). *Understanding by design* (2nd ed.). Alexandria, VA: ASCD.

Wilhelm, J. D. (2001). Think-alouds boost reading comprehension. *Instructor, 111*(4), 26–28.

Winter, J. (2002). *Frida.* New York: Arthur A. Levine.

Wood, A. (2009). *The napping house.* San Diego: Harcourt Brace.

Wood, D., Bruner, J. S., & Ross, G. (1976). The role of tutoring in problem solving. *Journal of Child Psychology and Psychiatry, 17*(2), 89–100.

Wood, D., & Wood, H. (1996). Vygotsky, tutoring and learning. *Oxford Review of Education, 22*(1), 5–16.

Yeager, D., & Dweck, C. (2012). Mindsets that promote resilience: When students believe that personal characteristics can be developed. *Educational Psychologist, 47*(4), 302–314.

Index

CORWIN

A SAGE Company

The Corwin logo—a raven striding across an open book—represents the union of courage and learning. Corwin is committed to improving education for all learners by publishing books and other professional development resources for those serving the field of PreK–12 education. By providing practical, hands-on materials, Corwin continues to carry out the promise of its motto: **"Helping Educators Do Their Work Better."**